People and Life 2

People and Life 2

Author Jack McBain
Publisher Chung Kyudo
Editors Kim Jinsuk, Cho Sangik, Kwak Bitna
Designers Park Bohee, Chung Kyuok

First Published July 2017
By Darakwon Inc.
Darakwon Bldg., 211, Munbal-ro, Paju-si, Gyeonggi-do 10881
Republic of Korea

Tel. 82-2-736-2031 (Ext. 550)

ISBN 978-89-277-0934-3 14740
978-89-277-0932-9 14740 (set)

http://www.darakwon.co.kr

Main Book / Free MP3 Available Online

12 11 10 9 8 7 6 25 26 27 28 29

People and Life 2

Introduction

People and Life 2 is the second book in a four-level series for adult and young adult learners of English. This dynamic series contains material appropriate for students ranging from a beginning level to an intermediate level. Each book in the series provides more challenging material in order to meet the linguistic needs of a diverse community of language learners.

People and Life 2 has 12 units, each of which consists of a warm-up, 4 supporting lessons, and a wrap-up, which serves as a review of the unit. The book covers a variety of topics set in a Western sociocultural context. Students will find topics such as friends, food, and hobbies interesting and relevant. Topics that are accessible and relevant to a student's life make learning English easier and more fun.

As a multi-skill course book, *People and Life 2* introduces essential everyday English with speaking, listening, writing, reading, grammar, and vocabulary sections. However, the speaking and listening sections have been emphasized due to the critical importance of these two language skills. *People and Life 2* offers numerous opportunities for students to engage in conversations and participate in activities in English. Through these interactive, confidence-gaining, and interesting activities, students can develop their communication skills and make progress toward greater competence in English.

Author's Acknowledgments

The author would like to express his most sincere gratitude to the editor Ms. Jinsuk Kim. Without her tireless work and guidance, this project would not have been possible. He would also like to acknowledge the contributions of the Darakwon management and staff. Finally, he would like to extend a heartfelt thanks to his family, who have been incredibly patient during the writing process of this book.

Scope and Sequence

Unit	Learning Outcomes	Speaking
Unit 1 These Days p.11 It's nice to see you again. I was just watching TV. What do you want to do? My Job Routine	*Students can . . .* make small talk talk about what they are doing now and what they were doing in the past talk about routines	Activities during the week Talking about hobbies Happiness chart Talking about work or school
Unit 2 Then and Now p.21 There used to be a school here. My Hometown Now I'm used to living alone. My new neighborhood is very different.	*Students can . . .* talk about past routines say what they did in the past talk about things they are used to doing now	What I do or used to do for fun Describing what you did in the past
Unit 3 People I Know p.31 Whose watch is this? Is this yours? I'm really excited! My BFF	*Students can . . .* describe positive and negative personality traits talk about the possession of objects describe their feelings and the reasons for their feelings	Personality traits Describing your favorite restaurant Describing your best friend
Unit 4 Different Cultures p.41 Meet My Parents You have to use two hands. Rules are rules. A Year of Teaching Abroad	*Students can . . .* talk about culture and etiquette talk about responsibilities talk about things that are prohibited talk about workplace rules	Polite and rude behavior Things you must do and don't have to do this week Hotel rules
Unit 5 A Slice of Life p.51 Do you want to play kick volleyball? It's organic! I'm afraid of flying. Grow some herbs!	*Students can . . .* describe the rules of a game give instructions say how they feel about various activities talk about their fears	Likes and dislikes Fears
Unit 6 Famous People p.61 Look! There he is. I need to memorize this. Famous Families The Hollywood Walk of Fame	*Students can . . .* compare people and things talk about types of entertainment	Making comparisons Listing words related to entertainment Saying something about Hollywood stars

Grammar	Listening	Vocabulary	Reading / Writing
Present simple Past simple Present continuous Past continuous	School subjects What were they doing? Activities you want to do	Activities and hobbies	**Reading** Job routines **Writing** Weekly routine
Past simple *Used to* *Be used to*	When the players were young His old house and his new house Past bad habits	Household chores	**Reading** Old and new neighborhoods **Writing** Bad habits you used to have
Whose and *who's* Possessive pronouns Adjectives	Whose items are these? What do you want to do?	Personalities	**Reading** *My BFF* **Writing** Your best friend
Must *Have to* *Don't have to* *Must not*	Actions and responses To-do list	Gestures Hotel rules and regulations	**Reading** Teaching abroad **Writing** Something you must do and must not do
Prepositions Gerunds and infinitives	The board game Maddie's life What are you afraid of?	Common fears	**Reading** An herb garden **Writing** Something you love and hate doing
Comparative adjectives Superlative adjectives	A famous conductor The Jackson Five Famous female singers	Entertainment	**Reading** A Hollywood trip **Writing** Comparing yourself to other people

Unit	Learning Outcomes	Speaking
Unit 7 Accidents p.71 Where are you? I've been in a car accident. Can't we go back? Ouch! I cut my finger. Look at my car!	*Students can . . .* talk about accidents talk about good and bad things that have happened to them talk about their experiences	Saying what has just happened Have you ever . . . ?
Unit 8 What would you do? p.81 A Promotion What would you buy? Muscles use a lot of energy. Murphy's Law	*Students can . . .* talk about future conditions talk about hypothetical situations talk about general truths	Future conditions Hypotheticals Applying Murphy's Law
Unit 9 Innovators p.91 Who was it invented by? My Favorite Book Solar Energy I am my own boss.	*Students can . . .* talk about famous inventors talk about their favorite authors and directors talk about new technology	Listing famous inventions and inventors A break-in and stolen things Interesting facts
Unit 10 Gadgets and Technology p.101 New Phone I lived in Paris for two years. I had already bought this one. Video Games and the Future of Gaming Your Most Important Possession	*Students can . . .* talk about technology talk about how long they have had an object talk about an action that had occurred before another action in the past occurred make a complaint talk about their most prized possessions	Old and new technology How long have you had . . . ? Past events A favorite item
Unit 11 I'm Stressed p.111 I'll help you. The Honeymoon I'll be living in Canada. A Record Deal	*Students can . . .* talk about stressful events talk about future plans and events make offers make promises make predictions about things that might be happening in the future	Offering help Making weekend plans for a visitor Talking about New Year's resolutions Predicting activities in 2050
Unit 12 Big Life Changes p.121 Driving in a New City Our New House You'll Get Over It Tim's Tiny House	*Students can . . .* talk about the manner in which they do things talk about where and when they do things	How do you usually . . . ? Describing activities in a two-story house Describing indoor and outdoor activities Making a list to improve the environment

Grammar	Listening	Vocabulary	Reading / Writing
Present perfect Phrasal verbs with *Go*	A recent injury Bitten by an animal An accident in the kitchen		**Reading** A car accident **Writing** An accident you have experienced
1st conditional 2nd conditional Zero conditional	Conversations about future conditions What would you wish for? A surprise	Super powers	**Reading** *Murphy's Law* **Writing** If you won a million dollars . . .
The passive voice	Famous modern artists A police report Three experiences	Interesting jobs	**Reading** Freelancing **Writing** Your job
Present perfect Past simple Present perfect Past perfect	A problem with the TV Relationships Customer service	Technological items Romance words and expressions	**Reading** The future of gaming **Writing** Your most prized possession
Future tenses Future continuous	Nervous about an interview A New Year's resolution In the future	Stressful events	**Reading** *A Record Deal* **Writing** A promotional article
Adverbs of manner Adverbs of place and time Phrasal verbs with *Get*	A new city Moving New to India	Manners Places Times	**Reading** A tiny house **Writing** How to improve the environment

Getting Ready

Let's learn some useful classroom sentences.

Your teacher says . . .

Raise your hand.
Open your book.
Write this down.
Find a partner.
Turn to page (page number).
Work in groups of (number).

Students say . . .

I don't understand.
Could you repeat that, please?
Speak more slowly, please.
How do I say (word, phrase, expression) in (language)?
How do you spell (word)?

Unit 1

These Days

Warm-up

Read the group chat messages. Then write the names that match the pictures.

Today

7:12 P.M.

Hey, guys! Are you staying busy during the semester break?

Peter Harris 7:13 P.M.

Not really. I just hang out with my friends on the weekend.

Mary Ellen 7:13 P.M.

I joined a gym. I lift weights three times a week.

Emily Jackson 7:15 P.M.

My friends and I sing karaoke on Friday nights. Join us!

Kate Tripper 7:16 P.M.

I study in the evenings. :(

Amy Holiday 7:20 P.M.

I go hiking on Saturdays. Why don't you come along?

Dave Winston 7:22 P.M.

I work in my garden every day. But I am free for karaoke on Friday night.

1.

2.

3.

4.

5.

6.

It's nice to see you again.

Conversation

Listen and practice the conversation. 01-01

A Hey, Pat. It's nice to see you again. How was your winter break?
B It was great, Samantha. I went to Mexico.
A Mexico? Why did you go there?
B I volunteered there. We built an elementary school.
A That sounds great.
B It was. How about you? What did you do?
A I went home for the break.
B That sounds nice. Did you spend time with your family and friends?
A Yeah, I did on the weekends. I was busy during the week. I worked at a nice restaurant. It was hard work, but I made a lot of money.
B Oh, cool!

TIPS & TIPS

It's nice to **meet** you. (Say this the first time you meet someone.)
It's nice to **see** you (again). (Say this when you see the person again.)

Grammar | Present Simple and Past Simple

A Let's learn about the present simple and past simple tenses.

Present Simple	Past Simple
Use this tense for routines, habits, things you do regularly, etc.	Use this tense for activities that are already completed.
I **study** English on Tuesdays and Thursdays. Junhee **doesn't eat** breakfast every morning. **Do** Tom and Yuki **travel** every summer?	I **ate** breakfast this morning. Franklin and Charles **didn't go** to Canada last year. **Did** April **have** a good time at the party yesterday?

B Complete the sentences with the correct forms of the present and past simple tenses.

1. He ______________________ class on Fridays. (not / have)
2. Mira ____________ to the store yesterday. (go)
3. I ____________ around Asia last summer. (travel)
4. We ____________ three times a week. (exercise)
5. Janie ____________ her teeth after every meal. (brush)
6. The teacher ______________________ Carolyn in class last week. (not / see)
7. Do you ____________ the guitar every day? (practice)
8. Where did Annabeth ____________ last weekend? (go)

Listening

A Listen to the conversation and answer the questions. 01-02

1. Who are the speakers?
   a. professors
   b. office workers
   c. students

2. What are the speakers talking about?
   a. their classes
   b. their teachers
   c. their vacation

3. Which subject does Tisa need help with?
   a. chemistry
   b. writing
   c. biology

B Listen again and choose True or False.

1. Yoshi hates his writing class. [True / False]
2. Tisa thinks chemistry is easy. [True / False]
3. Yoshi doesn't have any classes before noon. [True / False]

Pair Work

A Unscramble the words to make correct questions. Then write the questions in the table.

1. is / name / your / what
2. job / your / what / is
3. do / you / what / do / week / the / during
4. the / weekend / do / what / do / you / on
5. break / was / how / your
6. go / did / you / where
7. did / you / what / do
8. stay / long / how / there / did / you

	Questions	Answers
1		
2		
3		
4		
5		
6		
7		
8		

B Ask your partner the questions in the table. Then write your partner's answers.

I was just watching TV.

Conversation

Listen and practice the conversation. 01-03

A Isn't this a great concert?
B Yeah. The Buzzards are my favorite band.
A Mine, too. What were you doing when I called you this evening?
B Nothing much. I was just watching TV.
A Oh, because I called you twice, you know.
B Really? When did you call me the first time?
A Well, I called you at 6:00 p.m., but your phone was busy.
B I'm sorry. I was talking with my boyfriend. We were arguing when you called me the first time.
A What were you arguing about?
B He thinks I go out with my friends too much. He's a little jealous.
A Oh, that's funny.
B Why is it funny?
A Because you're out with me right now, silly!

Grammar | Present Continuous and Past Continuous

A Let's learn about the present continuous and past continuous tenses.

Present Continuous	Past Continuous
I **am watching** television. Philip **is eating** dinner with his family at the moment. Look! My cousins **are playing** in the yard. Alex and Wilbur **are talking** on the phone right now. You **aren't playing** tennis very well today. **Are** you **listening** to me? What **are** the students **doing** now?	The food **was getting** cold. We **were studying** English at 8:00 p.m. yesterday. I **wasn't listening** to music. Some of the students **weren't cleaning** their classroom at 5:30 p.m. **Was** Kevin **taking** a shower when the phone rang? What **were** you **doing** yesterday at 10:00 a.m.?

B Complete the sentences with the correct forms of the present and past continuous tenses.

1. Tom ______________ a movie now. (watch)
2. Ginny ______________ at 11:00 this morning. (sleep)
3. Isabelle ______________ for a test at the moment. (study)
4. Samir ______________ the bus to school when I called him. (take)
5. I ______________ when she texted me. (drive)
6. It ______________. Be careful! (rain)

7. What ________ she ________________ at 7:00 a.m. yesterday? (do)

8. ________ you ________ lunch now? (eat)

9. It ________________ when we left the theater. (snow)

10. They ________________ to work right now. (drive)

Listening

A Listen to Neil, Devon, and Byron. Then write the names in the correct places. 01-04

1. 

____

2. 

____

3. 

____

B Listen again and choose the correct words.

1. Neil's son was playing hockey at 11:00 a.m. on (Sunday / Saturday).
2. Devon was talking on the phone to (his boss / his customer) at 9:00 a.m. today.
3. Byron was (looking for a job / playing video games) this morning.

Class Activity

A Find out how many students were doing the activities in the table at these times.

Who was . . .	Number of Students
sleep / 6:00 this morning	
watch TV / 8:00 p.m. yesterday	
exercise / 6:00 p.m. yesterday	
eat a snack / 4:00 p.m. yesterday	
eat lunch / 12:00 p.m. yesterday	

B Answer the questions about the survey.

1. What was the most common activity?
2. What was the least common activity?

What do you want to do?

Conversation

Listen and practice the conversation. 01-05

A Which day is your favorite day of the week, Brian?
B Well, I love Fridays.
A Why's that?
B Because it's the last day of the work week. And I usually go to the movies on Friday nights. How about you, Jolene?
A I like Mondays.
B Are you serious?
A Yes, I am. I work out on Monday mornings. It puts me in a great mood. Why don't you join me this Monday?
B No, thanks. I will hate Mondays even more then.

Vocabulary | Activities and Hobbies

A Write the phrases in the correct places.

practice the trumpet	do judo	bake a cake
sing karaoke	drink in a bar	play video games

1.  ______________
2.  ______________
3.  ______________
4.  ______________
5.  ______________
6.  ______________

B What other activities do you do during the week?

I love to sing karaoke. I go to a karaoke bar with my friends once a week. On Sundays, I bake with my mother. We bake chocolate cakes . . .

Listening

A Listen to the telephone conversation. Then check the activities you hear. 01-06

B Listen again and choose True or False.

1. The man and the woman want to sing karaoke at a bar. [True / False]
2. The woman wants to do their usual activities this weekend. [True / False]
3. The man and the woman would like to play tennis this weekend. [True / False]
4. There is a tennis court near the man's house. [True / False]

Pair Work

A How do you feel on each day of the week? Make dots on the table. Then connect the dots to make a graph.

My Happiness Chart

	Mon	Tue	Wed	Thu	Fri	Sat	Sun

B Compare your chart with your partner's. Then ask questions about his or her week.

A Why are you very happy on Tuesday?
B Because I study English on Tuesday. I love my English class!

My Job Routine

Reading

A Read about three people's routines. 01-07

Chao is an office worker. He starts work at 8:00 a.m. and finishes at 7:00 p.m. He eats lunch and dinner in the company cafeteria. He doesn't eat breakfast. He prefers to sleep instead. On the weekend, he goes to the park with his wife and daughter. He and his wife occasionally go to the movies. Chao's mother sometimes babysits their daughter.

17 people like this. Like · Comment · Share

Write a comment . . .

Mikayla is a professional photographer. She works for a fashion magazine in Kiev, Ukraine. On the weekend, she likes to go hiking. She always brings her camera when she goes hiking. She takes beautiful pictures of the lakes and mountains, but she doesn't sell them. She posts them on her blog. Nature photography is just her hobby.

30 people like this. Like · Comment · Share

Write a comment . . .

Rene is a firefighter in New York City. As a child, she always wanted to be a firefighter. Last year, she graduated from the firefighter academy and became a real firefighter. She loves her job, but she doesn't like the hours. Sometimes she stays up all night and sleeps all day. She thinks it is strange to eat dinner when everybody else is eating breakfast.

52 people like this. Like · Comment · Share

Write a comment . . .

Comprehension Check **Answer the questions about the articles.**

1. Where does Chao usually eat lunch and dinner?
2. Why doesn't Chao eat breakfast?
3. Where does Mikayla post her pictures of lakes and mountains?
4. Which person's hobby is the same as his or her job?
5. What doesn't Rene like about being a firefighter?

B **Which of the three jobs do you want to do? Why?**

I want to be a firefighter. It is exciting and scary . . .

Listening

A Listen to the talks and answer the questions. 01-08

1. Who does Lars live with?
   a. his wife   b. his parents   c. his dog
2. What does Lars's mother tell her son to do?
   a. get a job   b. go back to school   c. clean his room
3. How big is Jean's bakery?
   a. small   b. medium-sized   c. large
4. What does Jean usually do at her workplace?
   a. answers the phone   b. cleans the floors   c. washes the windows
5. Why is Milan stressed at work?
   a. He is bored.   b. He hates his boss.   c. People give him more work.
6. Why can't Milan quit his job?
   a. He needs the money.   b. He works for his father.   c. He can't find a new job.

B Listen again and choose the correct words.

1. Lars is (27 / 28) years old, and his life isn't very (stressful / boring).
2. Jean (owns / doesn't own) her own (restaurant / bakery).
3. Lars is really (relaxed / stressed), and he (wants / doesn't want) to quit his job.

Pair Work

Talk about your job or school with your partner. How do you feel about it?

A How do you feel about your job?

B My job isn't very exciting, but I like it. I don't have to work on the weekend.

Writing

Think about your weekly routine. What is your week like? What are the good points and bad points? Then read your essay to the class.

My week is pretty normal. I go to work at 8:00 a.m., and I come home at 6:00 p.m. I am a manager, so my job is a little stressful. In the evening, I enjoy eating dinner with my family. My wife is a really good cook. On the weekend, I play board games with my children. Sometimes we go to the movies.

Wrap-up

A **Complete the sentences with the correct forms of the present and past simple tenses.**

1. I ____________ basketball with my friend yesterday. (play)
2. Shelly ________________________ breakfast this morning. (not / eat)
3. What do you ____________ on Wednesdays? (do)
4. Do you ____________ English? (study)
5. Naoki ____________ to Europe in the summer. (travel)
6. I ____________ to Alaska last year. (go)

B **Complete the sentences with the correct forms of the present and past continuous tenses.**

1. I ________________________ when you called me. (sleep)
2. Kerrie ________________________ to school now. (drive)
3. Why ____________ you ________________________ yesterday at 10:00 a.m.? (not / work)
4. ____________ he ____________ ? (smoke)
5. What ____________ he ________________________ at 6:00 p.m. last Tuesday? (do)
6. ____________ Philip ____________ French now? (study)

C **Talk about your happy day(s) of the week with your partner.**

A When do you feel happy?
B I feel happy on Fridays.
A Why?
B Because I usually go out with my friends in the evening.

D **What activities do your family members do during the week? When do they do them? Who do they do them with?**

Unit 2

Then and Now

Warm-up

A Look at the pictures. Which ones remind you of your hometown? Then say three things about your hometown.

1.

2.

3.

4.

5.

6.

B Look at the two pictures of Ken. What did he look like 17 years ago? How about now?

17 years ago
(He was 8 years old.)

Now
(He is 25 years old.)

There used to be a school here.

Conversation

Listen and practice the conversation. 02-01

A That's my old school.
B Wow. It's so big.
A It used to be really small. There were only eight students in my class. And there used to be a library next to the school.
B What happened to the library?
A It's a gym now. And that area over there used to be a park. We played sports there. Now it's an expensive apartment building.
B Wow. Your hometown used to be very different.
A I know. It used to be a small town. But it isn't small any more.

Grammar | Past Simple and *Used to*

A Let's learn about the past simple tense and the phrase *used to*.

Past Simple	*Used to*
Use this tense for actions or events that started and finished in the past.	Use this phrase for actions that happened regularly in the past but no longer happen.
I **played** tennis yesterday. I **didn't go** to school last Tuesday. **Did** you **see** a movie last week? – No, I didn't. Where **did** you **go** to high school? – I went to White Bear Lake High School.	I **used to** be short, but I am tall now. Albert **did not use to** like vegetables. **Did** you **use to** live in Auckland? - Yes, I did. Now I live in Christchurch. **Where did** Jonathon **use to** study? - He **used to** study in the library.

B Complete the sentences with the phrase *used to*.

1. We ____________________ video games. (play)
2. The birds ____________________ into the yard. (not / come)
3. I ____________________ a piano in my house. (not / have)
4. Where ________ they ____________ together? (go)
5. Sally ____________________ in ghosts. (believe)
6. Why ________ Suzie ____________ fish? (dislike)
7. They ____________________ best friends. (be)
8. Where ________ the Wilsons ____________ on the weekend? (go)

C What do you do for fun now? What did you use to do for fun when you were ten years old?

Listening

A Listen to the conversations. Write the correct names in the blanks. 02-02

Christy Webb Victoria Joseph Pete

B Listen again and choose True or False.

1. Joseph used to be really slow. [True / False]
2. Christy used to be a midfielder. [True / False]
3. Webb used to be a striker. [True / False]
4. Victoria used to catch the ball well. [True / False]
5. Pete is the speaker's big brother. [True / False]

Group Work

A Ask your group members one thing they used to do as children. Then write the answers in the table.

	Name	What did you use to do as a child?
1		
2		
3		
4		
5		

A What did you use to do as a child?
B I used to play video games.

B Did any of the members have the same answers? If yes, what was it?

John used to play video games. Felicia used to play video games, too.

My Hometown

Conversation

Listen and practice the conversation. 02-03

A How often do you visit your hometown?
B I live far from my hometown. So I go back about once a year.
A When did you go back the last time?
B I went back home about six months ago. It was really fun.
A What did you do?
B I spent time with my family. They still live there.
A I went home two years ago.
B Two years! Why did you wait so long?
A Flying home is really expensive. And most of my school friends moved away.
B Oh, I see. You should go back more often. Your parents probably miss you a lot.
A Yeah, you're right.

TIPS & TIPS Ago and Before

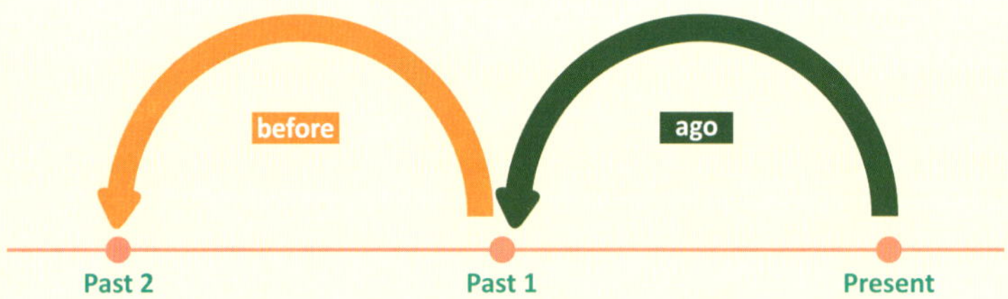

Sadie and Carolyn met three years **ago**. Lisa ate breakfast two hours **ago**.	Sadie and Carolyn lived in the same city **before** they met. Lisa ate a cookie **before** she ate breakfast.

Pair Work Write today's date in the timeline. Then ask your partner questions about Janette's life.

Janette's Life Since 2007

2007	2008	2009	2010	2011	2012	2013	2014	2015	. . .	Now
graduated from high school				graduated from college		met her husband	January / got married	April 6 / got a new job		Today's Date

A When did Janette meet her husband?
B She met her husband four years ago. / She graduated from college before she met her husband.

Listening

A Listen to the conversation and answer the questions. 02-04

a. 
b. 
c. 
d. 

1. Where does the man live now? Choose the correct picture.
2. Which house is the man's old house? Choose the correct picture.

B Listen again and answer the questions.

1. How many years ago did the man move into his house?
   a. one b. two c. three
2. What size house did the man use to live in?
   a. small b. medium c. big
3. What color was the man's old house?
   a. red b. brown c. yellow
4. What does the man like having at his new house?
   a. a veranda b. a garage c. a swimming pool

Speaking

Say what you did at these four times in the past.

ten years ago — five years ago — one year ago — six months ago — **Now**

I moved into a new apartment six months ago. I started a new job one year ago . . .

Pair Work

Ask your partner what he or she was doing at these times in the past.

12 hours ago	3 hours ago	30 minutes ago	5 minutes ago

A What were you doing five minutes ago?
B I was talking to Brian in the hallway.

Now I'm used to living alone.

Conversation

Listen and practice the conversation. 02-05

A Jessica, is that you?
B Hey, Chen. How are you doing?
A Really good. When did you move back?
B I didn't. I still live in Chicago. I'm just visiting here for a few days.
A I see. So how do you like Chicago?
B I like the city very much. But . . .
A But what?
B I didn't like living alone at first. Living alone was new to me.
A And now?
B I'm used to it now. But I'm still not used to doing all the household chores.

Grammar | *Be used to*

A Let's learn about the phrase *be used to*.

We grew up in the city. We **are used to** driving in bad traffic. Shelly moved to Seattle six months ago. She **is used to** the rainy weather now.	I moved to London two weeks ago. But **I'm not used to** driving on the left side of the road. Theresa and I are new roommates. We **are not used to** living together.
Are you **used to** cooking for yourself? - No, I'm not. I miss my mother's cooking. **Is** Luna **used to** going to college now? - Yes, **she's used to** the many homework assignments.	

* be used to = be accustomed to
I **am used to** getting up early. = I **am accustomed to** getting up early.

B Complete the sentences with the phrase *be used to*.

1. Naomi ______________________ up early for work. (get)
2. She ______________________ lots of homework. (not / have)
3. __________ Edwina ______________________ a big car? (drive)
4. Arthur and I ______________________ dinner late in the evening. (eat)
5. What exercises __________ you ______________________ at the gym? (do)
6. Zach and his partner ______________________ the piano three hours a day. (not / practice)

Vocabulary | Household Chores

dust the bookshelves

sweep the steps

vacuum the floor

feed the dog

scrub the sink

wash the windows

water the plants

take out the trash

mop the floor

Cheyenne **mops the floor** once a week.
Lisa **feeds the dog** every morning.
Simon often **waters the plants**.

Jack **takes out the trash** every day.
Jane **dusts the bookshelves** every month.
April **vacuums the floor** in her apartment.

Q. How often do you do these chores? What other chores do you know?

Class Activity

Play bingo with your classmates.

[Rules]

1. Everyone writes his or her name on a piece of paper and puts it in a box.
2. Everyone fills in each box on the Bingo card with household chores.
3. The teacher draws a name from the box and calls out the name.
4. The person with that name picks one chore.
5. Cross off the chore from the bingo card. The person who crosses off three chores in a row or column wins.

BINGO		
	Free	

My new neighborhood is very different.

Reading

A Read about Jason. 02-06

Where to Live

Country vs. City

My name is Jason, and I used to live in the country. There weren't that many people in my neighborhood. And I knew all the people on my street. In the summer, children played outside at the park. In the winter, they had snowball fights. I used to live in a big house. So I was used to having a lot of space. I had a large kitchen and several bathrooms and bedrooms in my house. And I used to have a garage and a car. I used to drive to work every day. I liked living in the country.

But now I live in the city, and it is very different. I live in an apartment, and there isn't much space. I'm not used to living in such a small place. I also share the small apartment with a roommate because rent is too expensive. The city is very noisy. I can always hear loud people, cars, and sirens. It is a little dangerous, too. Children don't play outside. They play inside. I take the subway to work now, too. There aren't any places to park a car.

Comprehension Check Answer the questions about the article.

1. Where did Jason use to live?
2. Where does he live now?
3. What did children use to do in the summer in his old neighborhood?
4. Where do children play in his new neighborhood?
5. How did Jason use to get to work?
6. How does he get to work now?

B What kind of neighborhood do you live in now? What kind of neighborhood did you use to live in?

Listening

A Listen to the three talks. Then choose the correct words. 02-07

1. The talks are about (bad habits / interesting hobbies).
2. Simone changed her habit because of her (mother / husband).
3. Jezebel was 16 years old when she (started / stopped) her habit.
4. Adelaide (changed / stopped) her habit.

B Listen again. Then draw lines to make true sentences about the speakers.

		d. one	
1. Simone used to	a. drink		j. hour(s) a day.
		e. two or three	
		f. five (or six)	
2. Jezebel used to	b. use her phone		k. pack(s) of cigarettes a day.
		g. ten	
		h. sixteen or seventeen	
3. Adelaide used to	c. smoke		l. cup(s) of coffee a day.
		i. twenty	

Writing

Write about a bad habit you used to have. Did you quit or change the habit? How did you do that?

Wrap-up

A Complete the sentences with the phrase *used to*.

1. Eileen ______________ in a small apartment. Now she lives in a house. (live)
2. Smith ______________ regularly. Now he works out three times a week. (not / exercise)
3. A What ________ you ______________ when you were overweight? (eat)
   B I ______________ a lot of junk food. (eat)
4. A Where ________ Simon ______________ to college? (go)
   B He ______________ to California University. (go)

B Complete the sentences with the phrase *be used to*.

1. Alex ______________ such late hours. (not / work)
2. Barbara ______________ a roommate. (have)
3. ______________ Arthur and Santiago ______________ far to work? (drive)
4. My friend and I ______________ in such a nice neighborhood. (not / live)
5. What games ________ you ______________ in class? (play)

C Read about Anthony's life. Then complete the chart with the correct information.

Anthony graduated from college ten years ago. He traveled for a year. Then, he got a job nine years ago. He bought a house five years ago. And one year ago, he got married. He started a new job six months ago. He is very happy with his life.

Anthony's life

now	
	He started a new job.
1 year ago	
	He bought a house.
10 years ago	

D What do you think are healthy habits? What healthy habits do you have?

Unit 3

People I Know

Warm-up

A Look at the pictures. Describe the people by using adjectives.

B Look at the pictures. What relationship do they have with one another? Why do you think so?

C Say your best friend's name and his or her job. Then say why you like him or her.

Whose watch is this?

Conversation

Listen and practice the conversation. 03-01

A Whose watch is this?

B Oh, it's Devon's.

A Who's he?

B He's my best friend. He visited me last weekend. I think he left it here.

A Tell me about him. What's he like?

B He's great. He's witty and charming. He's a doctor. What's your best friend like?

A She's intelligent and artistic. She's a painter. But she's also very sensitive.

B What do you guys do together?

A We watch romance movies. But she always cries at the end. It's so annoying!

TIPS & TIPS be like & like

What **is** he **like**?	(wants to know about a person's personality)
What does he **like**?	(wants to know what things or activities a person likes)
What does he look **like**?	(wants to know about a person's appearance)

Vocabulary | Personalities

A Look at the words and divide them into what you think are positive and negative personality traits.

rude	witty	annoying	artistic	charming
intelligent	polite	sensitive	curious	impolite

Positive Personality Traits:	Negative Personality Traits:

B Complete the sentences with the correct words.

1. Janine got an A+ on her exam. She is very ______________.
2. Shilo makes a very good first impression. He's a ______________ guy.
3. Esteban draws beautiful pictures. He is ______________.
4. June can be very ______________. Sometimes she doesn't even say hello to me.
5. He is really interested in new things. He's a ______________ person.

Grammar | *Whose* and *Who's*

A Let's learn about *whose* and *who's*.

Whose (possession)	**Who's = Who is** (contraction)
A **Whose** car is this? B It's Matt's car.	A **Who's** the man in the green hat? B That's George. He's a student here.
A **Whose** coins are these? B They're Sandra's coins.	A **Who's** the actor with the most money? B I think Tom Cruise is the actor with the most money.
A **Whose** keys are these? B I think they are Kate's keys.	A **Who's** coming to the party tonight? B Janet, Sujin, and Billy are coming.

B Complete the conversations with either *whose* or *who's*.

1. A ____________ hat is this?
   B It's Perry's hat.
2. A ____________ that?
   B It's Chantelle. She's Barry's girlfriend.
3. A ____________ the actor that was in the movie *The Wizard of Oz*?
   B It's Judy Garland.
4. A Do you know ____________ car is parked here?
   B I'm sorry. I don't know.
5. A I'm sorry, but I can't teach the class on Thursday.
   B ____________ going to teach us then?
   A Mr. Simmons is going to teach the class on Thursday.

Pair Work Look at the pictures. Practice the conversation with your partner by using *whose*.

1. Andrea / apple

2. Seth / scarf

3. Ruth / earrings

4. Randy / ball

A Whose apple is it?
B It's Andrea's apple.

Is this yours?

Conversation

Listen and practice the conversation. 03-02

A Hey, is this your biology book?
B No, that's yours.
A Oh, okay. How about this CD?
B I think it's mine.
A Okay, here you are.
B Hey, this old letter is yours.
A Let me see it. Oh, I wrote this to Mika Sandberg during my freshman year.
B Why didn't you give it to her?
A I was too shy.
B Too bad. She's dating Brad Fielder now.
A I know.

Grammar | Possessive Pronouns

A Let's learn about possessive pronouns.

singular	I – **mine**	you – **yours**	he – **his**	she – **hers**	it – **its**
plural	we – **ours**	you - **yours**		they – **theirs**	

These shoes are **his**.
Those sandals are not **mine**. They are **hers**.
This room is **ours**, and that room is **yours**.

TIPS & TIPS Name +'s

The book is **Paul's**.
These boxes are **John's and Sarah's**, but those boxes are not theirs.
cf. These boxes are **John and Sarah's**. (The boxes belong to both John and Sarah.)

B Complete the sentences with the correct possessive pronouns.

1. A Are these Monica's jeans?
   B Yes, they're ______________. (she)
2. A Whose guitar is this?
   B It's ______________. (me)
3. A Whose cards are these?
   B They aren't ______________. (we)
4. A Is this Andre's pencil case?
   B Yes, it's ______________. (he)
5. A Is this Becky and Pierre's car?
   B No, it isn't ______________. (they)
6. A Are these my keys?
   B Yes. They're ______________. (you)

C Say the chant. Use different possessive pronouns.

I have a bike. The bike is for me. It is my bike. The bike is mine.

You have pencils. The pencils are for you. They are your pencils. The pencils are yours.

Listening

A Listen to the conversations and check the words you hear. 03-03

☐ mine ☐ hers ☐ theirs ☐ yours ☐ his ☐ ours

B Listen again and answer the questions.

1. What kind of clothing did Jacob lose?
   a. a blue coat b. a red jacket c. a red T-shirt
2. What color is the phone?
   a. black b. silver c. brown
3. Whose SUV might it be?
   a. Jacob's b. Judith's c. Emily's
4. Where did the woman find the purse?
   a. in front of the sofa b. next to the sofa c. behind the sofa

Pair Work

Play the board game with your partner.

Rules

1. Put a marker on START. Any small items can be markers.
2. Flip a coin. Heads: move one space. Tails: move two spaces.
3. Look at the highlighted words. Complete the sentences by using the correct possessive pronouns.
   For example: *This is Mike's car. → The car is his.*

START	These are **Barbara's pictures**. → They are _____.	Where is your sandwich? → Where is _____?	Start Over	Are these my pancakes? → Are these _____?
				Free Space
Skip a Turn	This is not our English classroom. → It isn't _____.	Where is the dog's ball? → Where is _____ ball?	Move 2 Spaces Forward	That's Ken and Ben's house. → That's ____ house.
Sharon's car is new. My car is old. → _____ is new. _____ is old.				
Walter's and my friends are kind. → _____ are kind.	Move 2 Spaces Back	This is not Cindy's bedroom. → This is not _____.	That's Dustin and Frank's video game. → That's _____.	FINISH

Q. Who won? *I did. The victory is mine.*

I'm really excited!

Grammar | Adjectives

A Let's learn about *-ing*, and *-ed* adjectives.

-ing adjectives	*-ed* adjectives
boring, surprising, frightening, confusing, interesting, exciting, disappointing . . .	bored, surprised, frightened, confused, interested, excited, disappointed . . .
I hate this class. It is so **boring**. The movie was very scary. In fact, it was **frightening**. Learning math is difficult. It can be **confusing** for many people. This amusement park is an **exciting** place.	I'm so **bored**. This class isn't interesting. That was a scary movie. We were **frightened**. Kathy doesn't understand math. She is often **confused** in math class. Emily is **excited** to go to the amusement park.

B Look at the pictures and choose the correct words.

1. annoying / annoyed

2. disappointing / disappointed

3. shocking / shocked

C Choose the correct words.

1. The movie was very difficult to understand. My friends and I thought it was (confusing / confused).
2. Samantha bought a new dress for a party on Friday evening. She's very (exciting / excited).
3. The haunted house was (frightening / frightened). All of Joe's friends were (frightening / frightened).
4. We are not (interesting / interested) in poetry. We think poetry is really (boring / bored).
5. The directions to May's house were really (confusing / confused). My wife and I were (confusing / confused).

Listening

A **Listen and complete the conversation.** 03-04

A I'm bored. Let's ____________ that new documentary about jazz music.
B No, thanks. I'm not really ____________ in that.
A There's an ____________ art exhibit at the museum. Why don't we go there?
B I saw it ____________ weeks ago.
A Oh. We can see the new ____________. Brad Cochrane is in it. It looks ____________.
B I don't like his movies. He's ____________.
A Then what do you want to do?
B Let's play ____________. Space Fighter II is ____________.
A Okay. I guess we can do that.

B **Listen to the rest of the conversation. Then answer the questions.**

1. Why does the man stop playing the video game?
   a. He's bored. b. He's hungry. c. He's depressed.
2. Why doesn't the woman want to eat at the Italian restaurant?
   a. The place is depressing.
   b. The food is disgusting.
   c. The food is too expensive.
3. Why doesn't the woman want to eat at the Mexican restaurant?
   a. The restaurant is boring.
   b. The restaurant is depressing.
   c. The restaurant is disgusting.

Speaking

Describe your favorite restaurant. Give some reasons why you like it.

I like Mama's Tacos. It's a Mexican restaurant in my neighborhood. Its tacos are amazing. And the atmosphere is exciting. I love the music and the colors.

My BFF

Reading

Read about Anna's best friend. 03-05

I am Anna. Today, I would like to tell you about my BFF, or my "best friend forever." Her name is Farah. Farah means "joy" in the Hindi language. I think her name is perfect for her personality. She is such an amazing person. She is generous, sensitive, and witty. She makes me laugh so hard. She is very beautiful, too. She's tall, and she has long black hair. Her best feature is her big brown eyes.

She is from India, but her family moved to America fifteen years ago. I met her in elementary school. We were in the same class. She is a university student now. And she is studying to become a veterinarian. She really loves animals.

Now let me tell you why she is so special to me. About five years ago, I got really sick. I had to go to the hospital. Farah visited me every day. She gave me my homework and talked to me. Sometimes I was depressed and didn't want to talk to anybody. But she didn't mind. She just sat there in the hospital room with me. Farah is a great friend, and I love her a lot!

Comprehension Check Answer the questions about the article.

1. What does Farah's name mean?
2. What is Farah like?
3. What job does Farah want to do in the future?
4. Where is Farah's family from?
5. What does Farah look like?
6. Why is Farah a special friend to Anna?

Pair Work

Ask your partner some questions about his or her best friend.

A What's your best friend like?
B He's very generous. He always invites me to his house for dinner. And he's a great chef!

A What does your best friend look like?
B He's short and a little fat. He has brown hair, and he wears glasses.

Writing

A Complete the chart with information about your best friend.

My Best Friend	
Name	
Age	
Job/School	
Personality	
Physical Appearance	

B Write about your best friend. Use the information from the chart.

My best friend is ....

....

....

Presentation

A Tell the class about your best friend.

My best friend's name is Max. He is 22 years old. He is a senior at Capital University. He is quite charming and athletic. He runs marathons with his girlfriend. He is very handsome, and he is in great shape because he runs a lot.

B At the end of the presentation, let your classmates ask you questions about your best friend.

A Where did you meet your best friend?
B I met him in high school.
A Why do you like him?
B We both like sports. It's something we have in common.

Wrap-up

A Complete the sentences with *whose* or *who's*.

1. A _____________ office is that?
   B That's Ms. Simon's office.

2. A _____________ that?
   B It's Carol, Jacob's girlfriend.

3. A _____________ car is in front of my house?
   B I think it is Kevin's car.

4. A _____________ notebook is this?
   B Look inside. Maybe there's a name in it.

5. A I'm sorry, but Jerry can't come to your party.
   B _____________ going to come then?
   A Mitch, Young, and Chen are still coming.

B Complete the answers with the correct possessive pronouns.

1. A Are these Philip's papers?
   B Yes, they're _____________. (he)

2. A Whose ring is this?
   B It's _____________. (me)

3. A Whose cards are these?
   B They aren't _____________. (she)

4. A Is this their house?
   B No, it's not _____________. (they)

5. A Is this our package?
   B Yes, it's _____________. (we)

6. A Are these my shorts?
   B Yes, they're _____________. (you)

C What kind of a person are you? Describe your good points.

D Put the words in the correct places.

interested / interesting   frightened / frightening   boring / bored   confusing / confused

1. The book was long and difficult. I got really _____________.
2. The horror movie was _____________.
3. That was a terrible play. It was so long and _____________.
4. I really liked the teacher's lecture today. It was very _____________.

E Say who your favorite character in a novel or movie is. What does the character do in the story? Why do you like him or her?

Unit
4
Different Cultures

Warm-up

A What do you think about visiting a new country? What can be difficult about visiting a new country?

B Look at the pictures. Check the gesture when you know its meaning.

bow ☐

handshake ☐

wai ☐

wave ☐

high-five ☐

okay ☐

thumbs up ☐

salute ☐

C Which gestures do you use in your country? Are any of these gestures rude in your country?

Meet My Parents

Conversation

Listen and practice the conversation. 04-01

A Ian, I'm a little nervous about meeting your parents.
B Don't worry, June. Just say, "Nice to meet you, Mr. and Mrs. Miller," and then shake their hands.
A Shake their hands? We don't touch hands in my country.
B Relax. It's polite in America. And be sure to make eye contact.
A Make eye contact, too? I'm going to offend them.
B No, you won't.
A They're older than me. It's rude.
B Not in my country. We shake hands and make eye contact.
A I'll try, but I'm nervous.
B You'll do fine.

Group Work

A Rate the following examples from 1 (not rude) to 5 (very rude).

	Situations	1	2	3	4	5
1	You share a desk with an American coworker. When he is tired, he puts his feet on the desk.					
2	Your friend makes a lot of noise when she eats her noodles.					
3	A man spits on the subway platform when you are waiting for the train.					
4	A woman puts her bag in the empty seat next to her on the bus. You don't have a seat and must stand.					
5	Your friend invites you to dinner. When the bill comes, he asks you to pay half of the bill.					
6	Your friend visits your house. Without asking, he opens your refrigerator, takes out a can of soda, and drinks it.					
7	You tell your friend that you like a male classmate romantically. She tells several other students in the class.					

B Compare your answers with those of the other group members. Which example is the rudest?

Listening

A Listen to the talks. Then match the actions with the correct responses. 04-02

Actions		Responses	
1. 	•	• a.	
2. 	•	• b.	
3. 	•	• c.	

B Listen again and answer the questions.

1. Why did the man's boss become really angry?
   a. Pointing your feet at someone in Thailand is rude.
   b. It's rude to relax at work.
   c. The man said something rude to his boss.
2. Why was the man's grandmother happy?
   a. Her grandson's girlfriend was kind.
   b. Her grandson's girlfriend ate a lot of noodles.
   c. Her grandson's girlfriend ate the noodles loudly.
3. Why was the woman's sister embarrassed?
   a. A man bowed to her politely.
   b. A man kissed her.
   c. A man didn't like her.

Pair Work

A Make a list of three examples of polite behavior in your country. Then make a list of three examples of rude behavior.

Polite:	Rude:

B Compare your list with your partner's.

A Is talking while chewing gum a rude behavior in your country?
B Yes. Most people think so.

You have to use two hands.

Conversation

Listen and practice the conversation. 04-03

A I'm going to introduce you to my boss.
B Great. I can't wait to meet her.
A But you have to remember a few things.
B Like what?
A You have to bow. It's very polite.
B Okay. Anything else?
A Yes. You must use two hands to receive her business card.
B Two hands? Why can't I just take it with one hand and say thank you?
A In Japan, it's impolite to use one hand.
B Okay, so I should bow and receive her card with two hands. Got it!

Grammar | *Must* and *Have to*

A Let's learn about *must* and *have to*.

must	have to
You **must** be on time!	I **have to** call my sister tonight.
They **must** finish their work before 5:00 p.m.	Does Kerri **have to** attend the wedding?
Students **must** sign the attendance sheet.	The students **don't have to** attend class today.
Must you play your music so loudly? – Sorry. I'll turn it down.	**Do** you **have to** work on Saturday? – No, I don't.

TIPS & TIPS don't have to = don't need to

You **don't have to** go there. = You **don't need to** go there.

B Complete the sentences with *must*, *have to*, and *don't have to*.

1. Janine ________________ finish her work today.
2. Franklin ________________ meet with her boss today.
3. __________ we ________________ go to class today? It's snowing really heavily!
4. We ________________ work on Friday. It's a holiday!
5. They ________________ file the documents before the end of the day.
6. __________ I ________________ eat this old cheese? It smells terrible!

Listening

A Listen to the talk. Then complete the list by using the phrases in the box. 04-04

buy pasta, tomato sauce, and bread	call my mother
pay my rent	finish my chemistry report

To Do List

Must / Have to . . .

1. ____________________
2. ____________________
3. ____________________

Should

4. ____________________

B Listen again and choose True or False.

1. The man's report is due on Friday at midnight. [True / False]
2. The man is making dinner this evening. [True / False]
3. The man's rent was due yesterday. [True / False]
4. The man's mother's birthday is next week. [True / False]

Class Activity

Ask a classmate to tell you three things he or she has to/must do this week and three things he or she doesn't have to do this week. Write the answers in the table.

Student's Name	Have to / Must	Don't Have To

A What do you have to do this week?
B I have to buy a new coat.

A What don't you have to do?
B I don't have to go to work this week. I'm on vacation!

Rules are rules.

Conversation

Listen and practice the conversation. 04-05

A Ma'am, do you know why I stopped you?
B No, I don't.
A You were driving too fast. You must not drive over 60 kilometers per hour on this street.
B I'm sorry. I'm visiting this city, and I can't find my hotel.
A What hotel are you looking for?
B It's the Centerville Inn.
A Okay, take the first right. Then, go straight three blocks. It's on your right.
B Oh, thank you so much.
A I won't give you a ticket, but you have to slow down. It's dangerous to drive fast.
B Okay, I promise I will.

Grammar | *Must not*

A Let's learn about *must not* and *mustn't*.

You **must not** park here.

You **must not** enter the building by using this door.

You **must not** talk during class.

* You **mustn't** drive fast. (mustn't = must not)

B Look at the signs and write rules with *must not* or *mustn't*.

Example: 	*You must not take a video here.* (take a video)
1. 	______________________ (smoke)
2. 	______________________ (use a cell phone)
3. 	______________________ (speak)
4. 	______________________ (eat or drink)

Class Activity | The Hotel

A Find out what each picture and word or phrase means. You can use a dictionary, ask a classmate, or ask the teacher.

check in / check out

reception desk

receptionist

hotel lobby

hotel maid

hotel room

bill

room service

B Imagine your group owns a hotel. What are the rules for your guests? Write five rules by using *have to*, *don't have to, must,* and *must not*. Examples can include: check-in time, checkout time, smoking, visitors, breakfast time, costs for cancellation, and method of payment (cash/credit card/debit card).

	Hotel Name: ____________________
1.	*Guests must not smoke in the hotel rooms. They must go outside.*
2.	
3.	
4.	
5.	

C Now make three rules for your employees.

1.	*Employees must wear uniforms. / Employees don't have to wear uniforms.*
2.	
3.	

D Introduce your hotel to the class. Tell the class the name of the hotel and the rules for guests and employees.

Our hotel is called the Amazing Inn. Employees must wear white shirts and black pants. Guests mustn't check in before 11:00 a.m. . . .

A Year of Teaching Abroad

Reading

Read the newspaper column about the English teacher. 04-06

Tokyo Times Jan. 25

Culture Corner

This week, *the Tokyo Times* sat down with Jacob Miller, an English teacher from Los Angeles, California. We discussed living in Japan.

TT *Hi, Jacob. Thank you for talking with us today. How do you like Japan so far?*

JM I'm really enjoying my time in Japan. It's a beautiful country, and the people are super polite.

TT *I'm glad to hear that. What is difficult about living in Japan?*

JM Well, the language is really hard, so I study after work every day. I can't read yet, so I have to look at pictures when I order food at a restauarnt.

TT *That's funny! What do you think about Japanese customs?*

JM Japanese people are really nice. But there are so many rules for eating, working, and talking. For example, you must give and receive things with two hands. You also have to bow when you meet someone.

TT *Did you have any difficult experiences when you first came here?*

JM Yes. When I first met the Japanese teachers at my school, I thought they hated me.

TT *Why's that?*

JM They didn't make eye contact with me. They looked next to me or down and away from me. I thought they were hiding something.

TT *What were they hiding?*

JM Nothing. They were just being polite, but in a Japanese way. Too much eye contact is rude in Japan. Now we're all very good friends.

TT *Do you like teaching in Japan?*

JM Yes, I do. I really like my students. I love watching them get better at speaking English. I think I will stay for another year.

TT *That's great. Thanks for talking to us!*

Comprehension Check Answer the questions about the column.

1. How does Jacob Miller feel about Japanese people?
2. What is difficult for him in Japan?
3. What two rules about Japanese culture does he mention?
4. Why did the Japanese teachers not make a lot of eye contact with Jacob?

Writing

A What kinds of things must you do at your job? What kinds of things must you not do? Write them in the table.

I must . . .	I must not . . .

B Use the table to write a short essay about the things you must and must not do.

At work, I must ....

....

But I must not ....

....

Pair Work Make a list of four more jobs. Then ask your partner questions about the people who do these jobs by using *must*, *have to*, *mustn't*, and *don't have to*.

0	doctor
1	
2	
3	
4	

A What must a good doctor be?
B A good doctor must be very smart.

A What does a good basketball player have to do?
B A good basketball player has to score a lot of points.

Class Activity

Find someone who can say "yes" to these questions about work or school.

Do you have to ________ at work/school?	Name(s)
clean your desk	
wear a uniform	
arrive early	
sit a lot	
stay late	

A Do you have to sit a lot at work?
B Yes, I do. I sit all day long.

Wrap-up

A Write the words in the correct places.

wai bow wave handshake

1\.

____

2\.

____

3\.

____

4\.

____

B Fill in the blanks with *must*, *have to*, and *don't have to*.

1. You ____________ complete the project by Monday.
2. Will ____________ drive to work today. His mother is going to give him a ride.
3. We ____________ go to school today. It's a holiday.
4. Everyone ____________ bring a book and a pencil to class. They are necessary.
5. She ____________ pay the parking fee.

C Make rules for the signs with *must not* or *mustn't*. Then read them.

1\. 

2\. 

D Complete the sentences with your own opinions.

A best friend must ______________________________.

A good husband or wife must ______________________________.

A good boss has to ______________________________.

A good employee has to ______________________________.

A good teacher doesn't have to ______________________________.

A good student must ______________________________.

E Go online and find out which hotel is the most famous in your region. Then say three rules the hotel's guests must follow.

Unit
5
A Slice of Life

Warm-up

A What are the people in the pictures doing? Say the names of the activities.

B Look at the pictures above. Then complete the table.

I like . . .	I don't like . . .

Do you want to play kick volleyball?

Conversation

Listen and practice the conversation. 05-01

A Hey, Bora. Do you want to play kick volleyball on Saturday?
B Kick volleyball? What's that?
A It's a game my friends and I started playing a few months ago.
B How do you play?
A The rules are simple. Each team has two players. One team kicks the ball over the net, and the other team tries to kick it back.
B How do you score points?
A When a player kicks the ball into an area outside the lines, the other team gets a point. And when a player kicks the ball into the net, the other team gets a point.
B It sounds pretty easy.
A It is. So do you want to give it a try this Saturday?
B Sure. I'd love to.

Grammar | Prepositions

A Let's learn some prepositions.

into	up / down	over	inside / outside	toward

The man fell **into** the lake.
Paula ran **up** the hill
The ball rolled **down** the staircase.
The couple was sitting at a table **outside** the restaurant.
The train is coming **toward** the station.
Alex jumped **over** the puddle. He didn't want to get his shoes wet.

B Choose the correct prepositions.

1. She dropped the coin (into / up) the fountain.
2. We stayed at a guesthouse (outside / down) the city.
3. Suzie's skateboard rolled (up / down) the stairs after she fell off it.
4. The cyclists worked hard to go (up / outside) the hill.
5. Minsu waved and walked (up / toward) his group of friends.
6. The tennis players were very good. They hit balls (into / over) the net back and forth.

Listening

A Listen and choose the correct answer. 05-02

1. Which board game matches the game in the conversation?

a. 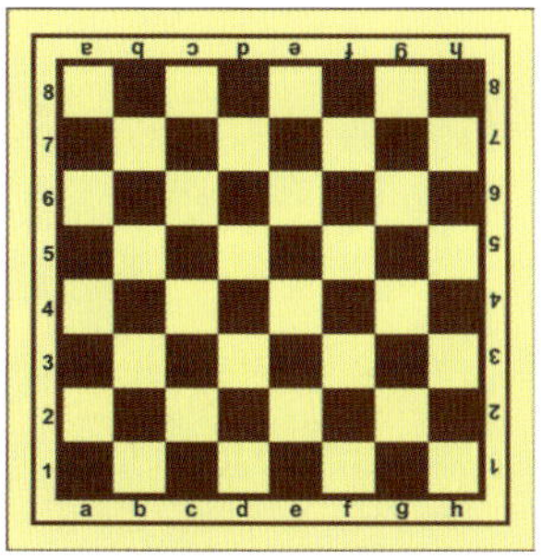

b. 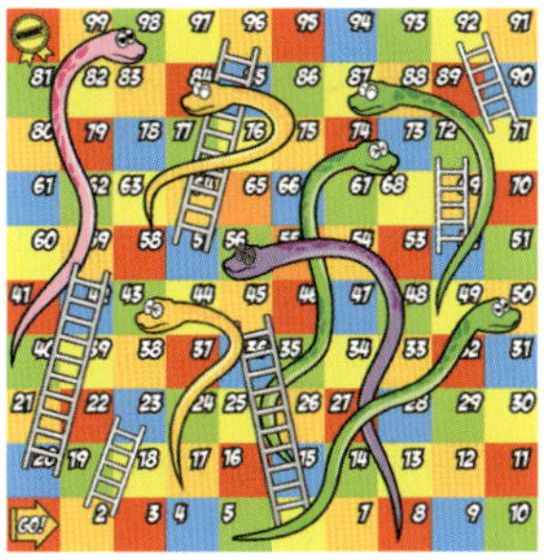

c. 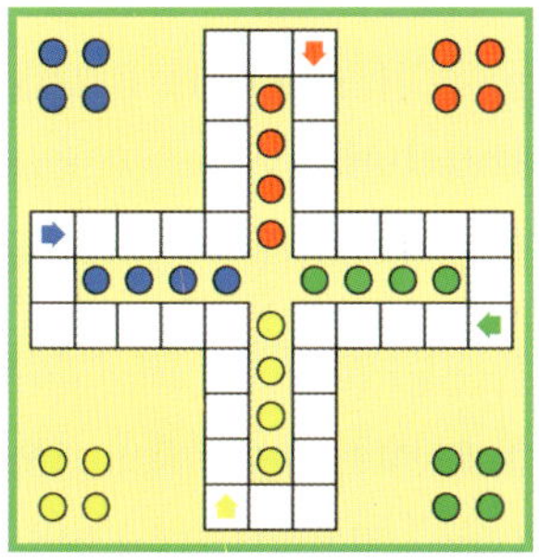

2. How do players move their game pieces up the board?

a. by flipping a coin b. by rolling a die c. by playing rock, scissors, paper

3. What happens when a player lands on a snake?

a. The player moves up. b. The player moves down. c. The player misses a turn.

4. Who wins the game?

a. the first player to land on a ladder
b. the first player to reach the 100th square
c. the first player to roll the die

B Listen again and choose True or False.

1. The man is teaching the woman how to play a new sport. [True / False]

2. Players start on the first square. [True / False]

3. Ladders are not good in Snakes and Ladders. [True / False]

Listening

A Place your pencil on Start. Then listen to the speaker and move your pencil through the maze. 05-03

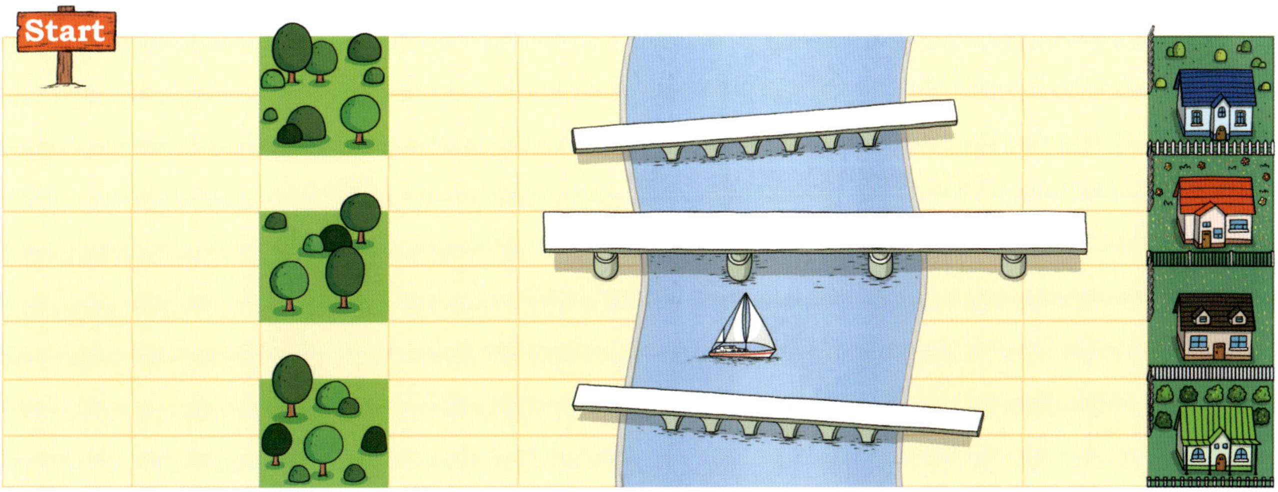

B Give your partner directions through the maze. Use a different path each time.

It's organic!

Conversation

Listen and practice the conversation. 05-04

A I'm glad to see you, Frank. I want to give you something.
B What's that?
A They're vegetables from my garden. I have too many, and I need to give some away.
B I didn't know you like gardening.
A Yeah, I love gardening. People say I am a good gardener.
B I agree. This lettuce looks amazing.
A It's organic, too.
B Really? I'm going to make a big, delicious salad tonight.
A In that case, let me give you some of these cherry tomatoes, too. They'll be great in your salad.
B Thanks a lot, Ginny.

Grammar | Gerunds and Infinitives

A Let's learn about gerunds and infinitives.

Gerund: verb + -ing	Infinitive: to + verb
the subject of a sentence **Jogging** is good for your health.	after adjectives It is fun **to play** basketball.
after a preposition Jodie thought about **calling** her ex-boyfriend.	the subject of a sentence **To read** before bedtime helps you fall asleep more quickly.
after some verbs: enjoy, like, love, hate Do they enjoy **singing**? They don't like **eating** fast food.	after some verbs: want, would like, need Do you want me **to call** you tonight? We need **to study** for the test.

B Complete each sentence with the correct gerund or infinitive.

1. Jane is worried about ____________ her bag at the concert. (lose)
2. Elliot and Sarah want me ____________ them this weekend. (call)
3. Do you need ____________ to the doctor? (go)
4. Jessica is afraid ____________ scary movies. (watch)
5. Is ____________ in a quiet neighborhood nice? (live)
6. Try not ____________ too quickly. You'll get a stomachache. (eat)

Listening

A Listen to Madison and answer the questions. 05-05

1. What is the topic of today's *Maddie's Life* podcast?
   a. things she doesn't like about the summer
   b. things she likes about the spring
   c. things she loves about the summer

2. Which activity does Madison talk about?
   a. eating b. swimming c. exercising

3. Who does Madison like to go to the beach with?
   a. her mother b. her boyfriend c. her best friend

B Listen again and choose True or False.

1. Madison has a recipe for homemade lemonade on her blog. [True / False]
2. Madison tells her fans to wear sunscreen. [True / False]
3. Madison loves to eat chocolate ice cream on a hot summer day. [True / False]

Class Activity

A Survey the class. Find out how the other students feel about the activities in the table.

How do your classmates feel about . . .	Love	Like	Don't Mind	Hate
drinking coffee				
exercising				
studying English				
drinking alcohol				
sleeping late				

A How do you feel about exercising?
B I hate exercising!

B Answer the questions about the survey.

1. Which activity do the students love doing the most?
2. Which activity do the students hate doing the most?
3. How many students hate drinking alcohol?
4. How many students don't mind sleeping late?

I'm afraid of flying.

Conversation

Listen and practice the conversation. 05-06

A What's that?

B It's just the jet engines. We're about to take off.

A I'm so scared. I am afraid of flying!

B I know. Just close your eyes and try to relax.

A Okay. What's happening now?

B We're moving down the runway.

A Oh, no!

B It's okay. We're off the ground now. We're flying.

A Are you sure we're going to be okay?

B I'm sure. You can open your eyes now. Everything's fine.

Vocabulary | Common Fears

A Put the words in the correct places.

flying going to the dentist mice water heights
small spaces spiders snakes public speaking

1.

2.

3.

4.

5.

6.

7.

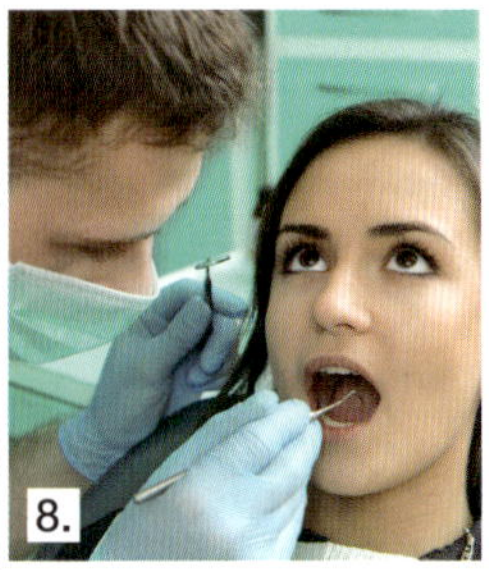
8.

9.

B Check the box if you have a fear of that item. Then say why you are afraid of it.

I have a fear of the water. I'm afraid of it because I cannot swim.

Listening

A Listen to the conversation and answer the questions. 05-07

1. Which dog looks like the dog in the woman's story?

a. 

b. 

c. 

2. Why does the woman have a fear of dogs?

a. A dog barked at her. b. A dog bit her. c. A dog followed her.

3. What do the woman's friends do with their dogs when she visits them?

a. They put their dogs in the backyard.

b. They ask their neighbor to watch their dogs.

c. They put their dogs in another room.

B Listen again and choose True or False.

1. A dog bit the woman on the arm when she was young. [True / False]
2. The woman starts shaking when she sees a dog. [True / False]
3. The woman thinks she will have a pet dog in the future. [True / False]
4. The woman wants to have a big dog as a pet. [True / False]

Group Work

Talk to your group members about your fears and some ways you can overcome them. Then complete the table.

Name	Fear	How I Plan to Overcome My Fear

I have a fear of flying. I hope to overcome it by taking a short trip on an airplane.

Grow some herbs!

Reading

A Read the online newsletter about gardening. 05-08

Carol's Corner Garden

Hey, readers! Welcome back to another week of Carol's Corner Garden. This is a weekly column for gardeners living in apartments or homes with small yards. When you only have a small amount of space, you have to think carefully about what to grow. This week, I want you to consider growing herbs. Herbs like basil and thyme can add so much flavor and excitement to your cooking. And they only need small pots to grow in. In addition to making your cooking better, herbs like mint can make you feel better when you are sick. If you have a stomachache, you can make a wonderful mint tea by adding dried mint leaves to hot water. Your stomachache will go away in no time. Let me share with you my three basic tips for taking care of an herb garden:

1. Water your herbs often after planting them. They need lots of water, especially in the first few days and weeks.

2. Make sure your herbs get plenty of sunlight. Put your plant boxes and pots near the window with the most sunlight. If you have a balcony, put them outside. Direct sunlight is necessary for growing healthy herbs.

3. Rotate your herbs. Make sure each side of your herb plant is getting regular sunlight. By rotating the pot, you can have better looking and better tasting herbs.

Well, that's all for today's Carol's Corner Garden. Read my column next week for your weekly gardening tips. Bye!

Comprehension Check Answer the questions about the online newsletter.

1. Why are herbs a good choice for apartment gardening?
2. Which herbs does she mention for cooking?
3. What kind of tea should you make if you have a stomachache?
4. What three tips does she give?
5. Why should gardeners rotate their herbs?

B Do you like gardening? Do you grow any vegetables, fruits, or herbs in your home?

Group Work

A Write about something you love doing. Why do you love doing it?

I love ....

....

B Write about something you hate doing. Why do you hate doing it?

I hate ....

....

C Read your essay to your group members. Make a list of the *loves* and *hates* in your group.

Name	Love	Hate

D Look at your group's list. Are any of the items on the list the same?

Wrap-up

A Circle the correct prepositions.

1. Don't go (over / into) the ocean! It's too cold.
2. Brad stepped (into / over) the puddle because he didn't want to get his shoes wet.
3. The couple drank coffee on the patio (toward / outside) the café.
4. The baby is walking (toward / down) his mother with his arms open.

B Choose the correct sentences.

1. a. Do they enjoy dancing?
   b. Do they enjoy to dance?
2. a. Sharon wants me to calling her tonight.
   b. Sharon wants me to call her tonight.
3. a. I would like Aaron stopping playing video games now.
   b. I would like Aaron to stop playing video games now.
4. a. Paul likes jogging with his friends.
   b. Paul likes to jogging with his friends.

C Read the email and answer the questions.

To	Sam_55@funmail.net
From	Lisa_23@happymail.com
Date	September 23
Subject	Trip to the Philippines

Dear Sam,

I'm sorry, but I cannot go with you to the Philippines this winter. I am afraid of flying. I went to a doctor to talk about my problem. The doctor told me to visit an airport just to look around. But when I got to the airport, my heart started beating really fast. And I started sweating. I couldn't breathe. I had to go home. At that moment, I knew I wasn't going to be able to go on a trip in an airplane. I really want to go with you, but I'm not ready to fly yet. Maybe someday. Sorry.

Lisa

1. What is the woman's fear?
2. Where does she want to go for winter vacation?
3. What happened when the woman went to the airport?

D Introduce a newspaper or magazine column you like to the class. You can copy and hand out one of the articles to your classmates. Say what the column is and why you like it.

Unit 6

Famous People

Warm-up

A Look at the pictures. What do these people want to be famous for?

B Make a list of famous people from your country for each category. Compare your list to your partner's list.

Movies / Film	Television	Theater	Music
______	______	______	______

C Why do people become famous? Do you want to be famous?

Look! There he is.

Conversation

Listen and practice the conversation. 06-01

A Oh! I see him.
B Where?
A Over there. Look! It's Landon Scarsdale. He's the world's most popular action movie hero.
B Is that really him? He's so short. He's shorter than I am.
A But he's so handsome.
B Really? He looks old. I think he's older than my dad.
A Come on! He's the star of *Shadow Master*. It's my favorite action movie.
B I know. He just looks a little smaller than he does in his movies.
A Don't be jealous. I still think you're more handsome.
B Thanks.

Grammar | Comparative and Superlative Adjectives

A Let's learn about comparative and superlative adjectives.

Comparative	the + Superlative
Braden is **older** than Ashley.	Braden is **the oldest** player on the team.
Mt. Everest is **bigger** than Mt. Kilimanjaro.	Mt. Everest is **the biggest** mountain in the world.
Robin is **funnier** than Jim.	Robin is **the funniest** student in our class.
Chemistry is **more interesting** than biology.	Chemistry is **the most interesting** subject.

* good – better – the best
far (distance) – farther – the farthest
bad – worse – the worst
far (quantity) – further – the furthest

B Complete the sentences with the correct comparative adjectives.

1. Mandy's boyfriend is ____________ than Sally's boyfriend. (tall)
2. The New York State Fair is ________________________ than the Alabama State Fair. (exciting)
3. Donald is ____________ than Richard. (funny)
4. This spring is ____________ than last spring. (wet)

C Complete the sentences with the correct superlative adjectives.

1. Who is the ____________ player in the National Basketball League? (short)
2. That was the ____________ meal. The chicken was disgusting. (bad)
3. I really like Brian. He's the ____________ among all my friends. (polite)
4. Bangkok is one of the ____________ cities in Asia. (hot)

D Look at the pictures and write true sentences about the six people.

Kate's brother / Kate

Jeremy / Jerome

Georgia / Janine

1. Kate's brother *is taller than Kate*. (tall / short)
2. Kate ____________________________.
3. Jeremy ____________________________. (poor / rich)
4. Jerome ____________________________.
5. Georgia ____________________________. (fat / healthy)
6. Janine ____________________________.

E Look at the pictures. Then make sentences by comparing the people in the pictures.

Albert
175cm, 70kg

Mitchell
188cm, 129kg

Arianna
169cm, 53kg

Albert is shorter than Mitchell.

Pair Work

Compare yourself to your partner. Who's taller? Older? Healthier?

A I'm 168 centimeters tall. How tall are you?

B I'm 177 centimeters tall. So I'm taller than you are.

I need to memorize this.

Conversation

Listen and practice the conversation. 06-02

A Ah! This is so difficult.
B What's the matter?
A I'm trying to memorize my lines for the play.
B What play is it?
A *Hamlet*.
B Ooh, Shakespeare. What part are you going to play?
A I'm going to play the part of Horatio, Hamlet's best friend.
B Do you want me to help you?
A Sure. Could you read Hamlet's lines?
B Of course, "Alas, poor Yorick. I knew him, Horatio . . ."

Vocabulary | Entertainment

A Put the words and phrases in the correct places.

audience	film director	ballerina	conductor
the cast	orchestra	musician	drummer

1.

2.

3.

4.

5.

6.

7.

8.

B Think of more words about the entertainment industry and write them.

Listening

A Listen and choose the correct answers. 06-03

1. What do the speakers think about Ming Chao's performance?
   a. It's terrible. b. It's incredible. c. It's pretty good.
2. What country is conductor Antonio Ferrara from?
   a. France b. Germany c. Italy
3. How old is the oldest conductor in the world?
   a. 92 b. 88 c. 82

B Listen again and choose True or False.

1. Ming Chao is the youngest violinist in the world. [True / False]
2. Antonio Ferrara is not the oldest conductor in the world. [True / False]
3. The oldest conductor in the world is from Germany. [True / False]

Pair Work

A Find the answers to the questions with your partner. You can use the Internet.

	Questions	Answers
1.	What's the most expensive diamond in the world?	
2.	What's the largest ocean?	
3.	What is the most populated city in the world?	
4.	What is the fastest land animal in the world?	
5.	What's the largest animal in the world?	
6.	What's the most polluted city in the world?	
7.	Who is the most famous actor in your country?	

A What is the tallest building in the world?
B Let me check on my smartphone. Here it is! Burj Khalifa is the tallest building in the world.

B Compare your answers with another pair's answers. Are they the same?

Famous Families

Conversation

Listen and complete the conversations. 06-04

1.

A I think Will Smith's family is the ____________ family in Hollywood.

B Really? Why do you think so?

A Everyone in his family acts in movies or makes music.

B I didn't know that.

A Will and Jaden even acted together in a sci-fi movie.

2.

A Do you know who the Hemsworth brothers are?

B Sure. Chris and Liam are in really ____________ action movies.

A Did you know they have another brother?

B No, I didn't.

A His name is Luke. He's ______________ Chris and Liam. But he stars in one of the most popular television series on TV.

3.

A Do you know who the Olson twins are?

B No, I don't.

A They were child actors in the 1980s and 90s. But now they are entrepreneurs.

B What do they sell?

A They sell ______________________________. They're very rich!

Listening

A Listen to the talk and check the words you hear. 06-05

☐ worldwide	☐ oldest	☐ album	☐ popular
☐ actors	☐ movies	☐ solo artist	☐ band

B Listen again and answer the questions.

1. When did the Jackson Five start?

   a. in the 1960s b. in the 1970s c. in the 1980s

2. Who was the most famous member of the Jackson Five?

   a. Tito Jackson b. Michael Jackson c. Janet Jackson

3. When did Michael Jackson become an international superstar?

   a. in the 1960s b. in the 1970s c. in the 1980s

Listening

A Listen to the conversation and answer the questions. 06-06

1. Who is the best singer according to the man?
   a. Lady Gaga
   b. Taylor Swift
   c. Katy Perry

2. Who is the most fashionable according to the woman?
   a. Lady Gaga
   b. Taylor Swift
   c. Katy Perry

3. Which one of the singers plays the piano well?
   a. Lady Gaga b. Taylor Swift c. Katy Perry

B Listen again and choose True or False.

1. The man doesn't think Katy Perry is a good singer. [True / False]
2. Taylor Swift writes her own music. [True / False]
3. The man thinks Lady Gaga is the most talented piano player. [True / False]
4. Katie Perry is taller than Taylor Swift. [True / False]

Pair Work

Ask and answer questions about the famous people by using comparative and superlative adjectives.

Name	Byung Hun Lee	Jackie Chan	Tom Cruise
Age	August 13, 1970	April 7, 1954	July 3, 1962
Height	177	174	170
Net Worth	$185 million	$395 million	$480 million
Nationality	Korean	Chinese	American

A Is Byung Hun Lee taller than Jackie Chan?
B Yes, he is. Byung Hun Lee is taller than Jackie Chan. Byung Hun Lee is the tallest.

The Hollywood Walk of Fame

Reading

Read about a trip to Hollywood. 06-07

My wife Monica and I are huge movie fans. This winter, we went to Hollywood in Los Angeles, California. We wanted to see where they make movies. We stayed in a big hotel on Sunset Boulevard. It had a great swimming pool, and there were lots of restaurants and bars within walking distance of the hotel. On the first day, my wife took a picture of the Hollywood sign. The next day, we went to Hollywood Boulevard. On the sidewalk, there were all these stars with famous people's names on them. Monica took a picture of Michael Jackson's star. On the third day, we took a tour of a movie studio. We got to see where they filmed some of our favorite movies and TV shows. On our last day, we went on a star maps tour. On this tour, a guide showed us famous people's houses. The houses were bigger than any of the houses in our city. We saw Britney Spears' and Lady Gaga's houses. Britney Spears' house was the biggest. But Monica thought Lady Gaga's house was more beautiful.

Comprehension Check **Answer the questions about the article.**

1. Why did the couple take a trip to Los Angeles?
2. What places were near the couple's hotel?
3. What did the couple do on their second day?
4. What did the couple do on their last day?
5. What did Monica think about Lady Gaga's house?

Class Activity

A Make groups of four or five students. Then compete with other groups for the gold medal in the Superlative Olympics. Add two more events in the empty spaces in the table.

The Superlative Olympics

Events	Name
Who is the tallest?	
Who has the shortest hair?	
Who can hold his or her breath the longest?	
Who has the largest feet?	
Who has the longest arms?	
Who is the youngest student?	

B Who won the most gold medals? Winner(s): ______________________

Writing

Compare yourself to other people. Use comparative and superlative adjectives to describe yourself and the others.

My brother and I are different. He is taller than I am. But I am thinner than he is. His hair is longer than my hair. My hair is darker than his hair . . .

Wrap-up

A **Complete the sentences with the correct comparative adjectives.**

1. The Burj Khalifa building is ____________ than the Empire State Building. (big)
2. My father is a banker, and my uncle is a musician. My uncle's job is ______________________ than my father's job. (exciting)
3. A Is Bangkok a ______________________ city than Singapore? (friendly)
   B Yes, it is.
4. Who is ____________: Edward or Alexandra? (polite)

B **Complete the sentences with the correct superlative adjectives.**

1. Mina is the ____________ student at my school. (smart)
2. Adventuretown Amusement Park is the ______________ amusement park in our country. (exciting)
3. A Is Cairo the ______________________ city in the world? (polluted)
   B No, it isn't.
4. Fred Smith is the ____________ actor in the world. (funny)

C **Make sentences about the people in the pictures by using comparative and superlative adjectives.**

Mary is taller than Albert. Paul is the tallest.

D **Write about an experience when you saw a famous person. Say the time and place and how you felt.**

Unit 7

Accidents

Warm-up

A Look at the pictures. Write the sentences in the correct places.

Ouch! A bee stung me.	Oh, no! I hit that car.
I cut my finger.	I hurt my leg playing soccer.
My ankle really hurts.	A snake bit my finger.

1.

2.

3.

4.

5.

6.

B Imagine you were in a small car accident. Complete the accident report with your information.

Accident Report			
1. Driver's Name			
2. Vehicle Type		3. Time	
4. Location			
5. License Plate Number			
6. Description of Accident			
		Signature:	

Where are you?

Conversation

Listen and practice the conversation. 07-01

A Princess! Princess! Excuse me, ma'am. But have you seen a small white dog recently?
B Yes, I have.
A Where did you see it?
B I saw it at the supermarket about ten minutes ago. It ran across the parking lot.
A What did it look like?
B It was small, and it was wearing a pink collar.
A That's her! Which supermarket were you at?
B I was at Jenkins Family Mart. It's on Highland and 2nd Street.
A I know where that is. Thank you so much!
B You're welcome.

Grammar | Present Perfect: Recent Actions

A Let's learn about the present perfect tense.

have + Past Participle
I've recently **visited** Rome. It was beautiful, but it was a little rainy. **Have** you **been** to the department store recently? – Yes, I have. Justin **has** recently **gotten** a new job in sales. He's very excited. My dog **has** recently **had** surgery. But she's going to be fine. Sammy **hasn't attended** English class recently.

B Complete the sentences with the correct forms of the present perfect tense.

1. Joan's mother ____________ recently ____________ a birthday. (have)
2. The Johnson's ________________________ a new house. (buy)
3. ____________ you recently ____________ to the market? (be)
4. What ____________ Annie ____________? (eat)
5. Lynn ________________________ a movie recently? (not / see)
6. They ________________________ Paris recently. (visit)
7. We ____________ just ____________ coffee there. (drink)
8. Where ____________ James ____________ tennis recently? (play)

Listening

A Listen to the talk and choose the correct answers. 07-02

1. What part of the man's body has he injured?
   a. his leg   b. his foot   c. his elbow
2. What has the man recently started learning?
   a. mountain climbing   b. tennis   c. skiing
3. How does the man describe himself?
   a. He is athletic.   b. He is impressed.   c. He is clumsy.

B Listen again and choose True or False.

1. Barbara climbed up and down the rock wall just fine. [True / False]
2. George fell off the rock wall. [True / False]
3. The woman thinks George will wear the cast for at least a week. [True / False]

Pair Work Look at the pictures. Ask your partner what has recently happened to the people.

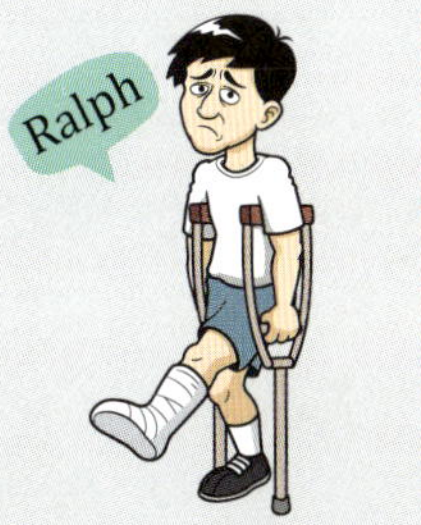

A What has happened to Ralph?
B He has recently broken his leg.

Speaking

A Look at the pictures. Say what has recently happened to the people.

1.

2.

3.

4.

He has recently won the lottery.

B Draw a picture of an event that has just happened. Then show the picture to your classmates and ask them what has just happened.

I've been in a car accident.

Conversation

Listen and practice the conversation. 07-03

A Have you ever been in a car accident, Carlos?
B Yes, I have.
A When did it happen?
B About two years ago. I was driving and texting at the same time.
A Oh, no. That's really bad.
B I know. It was really stupid.
A How hard did you hit the other car?
B Not very hard. It was just a small accident. How about you? Have you ever been in a car accident?
A No, I haven't. I'm really careful when I drive. And I definitely don't use my phone.
B I don't either these days.

Grammar | Present Perfect: Experiences

A Let's learn more about the present perfect tense.

have + Past Participle
Have you ever **visited** Hong Kong, Janet? – Yes, I have. I went there in 2009. Jun **has met** three famous people in his life. Erica **has** never **traveled** to Europe. **Has** he ever **eaten** Chinese food? – No, he hasn't. How many movies **have** you **seen** in 2017? - I've already seen 17 movies in 2017.

Janet was born. — Janet visited Hong Kong in 2009. — Now

B Complete the sentences with the correct form of the present perfect tense.

1. Fatima ____________ not ____________ to France yet. (not / be)
2. Selma ____________ already ____________ at the new restaurant. (eat)
3. They ____________ to many countries. (not / travel)
4. ____________ you ____________ chemistry yet? (study)
5. What kinds of music ____________ Adriana ____________ to? (listen)
6. ____________ we ever ____________ this place before? (visit)
7. Philip and Justin ____________ abroad. (live)
8. Kristi ____________ never ____________ anyone shorter than her. (date)

Listening

A Listen to the conversation and answer the questions. 07-04

1. A snake (has / hasn't) bitten the woman.
2. A water snake (has / hasn't) bitten the man.
3. The man (has / hasn't) had accidents when hiking.

B Listen again and answer the questions.

1. What bit the woman?
   a. a snake b. a dog c. a spider
2. What did the man do when he was bitten?
   a. He went to the hospital. b. He washed his leg with water. c. He ended his trip.
3. What can be inferred about the man?
   a. He doesn't like hiking. b. He often gets hurt. c. His father is a doctor.

Class Activity

A Complete the table with information about yourself.

Have you ever . . . ?	Yes	No
hurt yourself playing sports		
been bitten by a dog		
broken a bone		
stayed overnight in the hospital		
sprained your ankle		
had surgery		

B Share the results with your classmates.

I have broken a bone. I broke my arm playing softball. My friend hit me with a bat. It was an accident. She didn't see me.

Can't we go back?

Conversation

Listen and practice the conversation. 07-05

A Where are we?
B I know where we are.
A Are you sure? I'm worried. Can't we go back?
B Go back? I've hiked this mountain many times. We are almost at the top.
A My feet are sore. Why did I agree to go on this hike?
B Let's take a break and drink some water. Then, we can go on with the hike.
A Okay.
(ten minutes later)
B Now that you've had some water and rest, do you feel better?
A Yes, I do. I think I can go up a little farther.
B Okay, great. Let's do it!

Grammar | *Go*

A Let's learn about phrasal verbs with *go*.

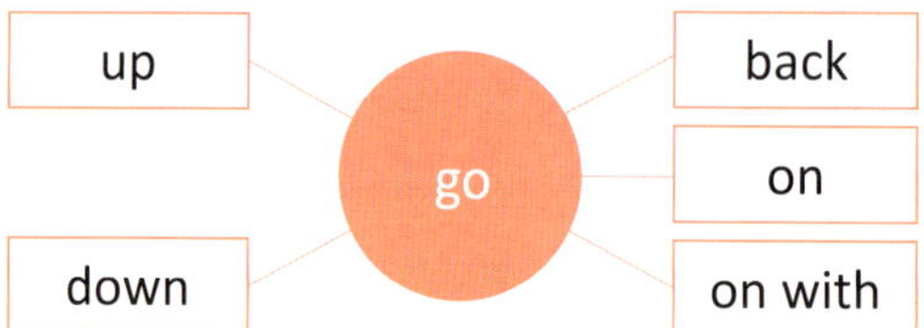

The children love to **go up** the ladder and down the slide at the park. (go up = rise, climb)
Julie left her smartphone at home. She decided not to **go back** and get it. (go back = return)
I wonder what's **going on** outside. (go on = happen, continue)
I don't think we should **go on with** the meeting. (go on with = continue with)
All the prices at the store **went down** after Christmas, so I saved a lot of money. (go down = fall, decrease)

B Complete the sentences with one of the following phrasal verbs: *go up, go back, go on, go on with*.

1. Should we ______________________ the elevator or the escalator?
2. I can't ______________________ this hike. I'm too tired!
3. I need to ______________________ home. I forgot my laptop.
4. Don't ______________________ a road trip in the winter. The snow on the roads is dangerous.

Ouch! I cut my finger.

Listening

A Listen to the conversation and choose the correct words. 07-06

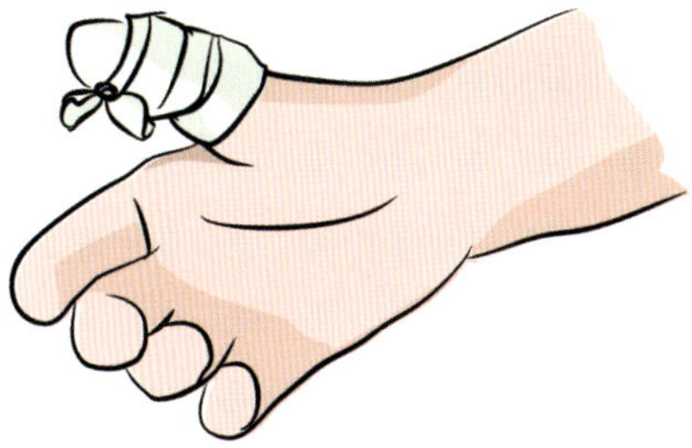

1. The woman was chopping some (carrots / tomatoes).
2. The woman cut her (arm / finger).
3. The woman put a (tissue / towel) on the cut.
4. The (man / woman) put on the bandage.

B Listen to the rest of the conversation and choose True or False.

1. The woman has cut her finger while cooking in the past. [True / False]
2. The woman can't finish making the soup. [True / False]
3. The man is going to cut the carrots. [True / False]
4. The woman's finger doesn't hurt at all. [True / False]

Class Activity | What Has Changed Game

Rules

1. Pick one person to be the changer.
2. The rest of the students must close their eyes.
3. The changer moves items to different locations in the classroom. For example, he or she moves the wastebasket from one side of the classroom to the other side.
4. When the changer finishes, the students find what has changed locations. Then, make a list.

	What has changed?
0.	*The wastebasket has changed locations. It used to be by the door. Now it's by the whiteboard.*
1.	
2.	
3.	
4.	
5.	
6.	
7.	

* Read your answers out loud. Who noticed the most changes?

Look at my car!

Reading

A Read the two emails. 07-07

To: jacob22@funmail.net
Date: August 3
Subject: an accident

Dear Jacob,

Let me tell you about my terrible day. I woke up late, so I was in a hurry. I didn't even eat breakfast. I decided to drink my coffee in the car on my way to work. But then I spilled hot coffee on my legs. I looked down, so I didn't see the car in front of me stop. And I hit it. There was a lot of damage to our cars. He was really angry. I told him I haven't been in an accident before. But he didn't listen to me. He just yelled at me. I called my insurance company. The agent told me it was 100% my fault because I hit him from behind. I'm so sad. I don't know what I'm going to do. My car is damaged, and now my monthly insurance payments are going to be really expensive. And look at my car. It's ruined!

Matilda

To: janine_95@handymail.net
Date: August 3
Subject: an accident

Dear Janine,

You'll never believe what happened to me today. A woman hit my car from behind. It was really scary. She was drinking coffee and not watching the road. Luckily, I didn't get hurt. And I don't have to pay any money. It was 100% her fault. But I was late for work because of the accident. Look at my car! What a bad day.

Simon

Comprehension Check Answer the questions about the emails.

1. Why was Matilda in a hurry?
2. Why didn't Matilda see Simon's car?
3. Was Matilda in the front car or the back car?
4. How did the man feel about the accident?
5. Whose fault was the accident?

B Have you ever been in a car accident? What happened? Whose fault was it?

I have been in a car accident. A man hit me from behind. I was okay, but my car had a little damage.

Writing

Write about an accident you have experienced. What happened? What did you do?

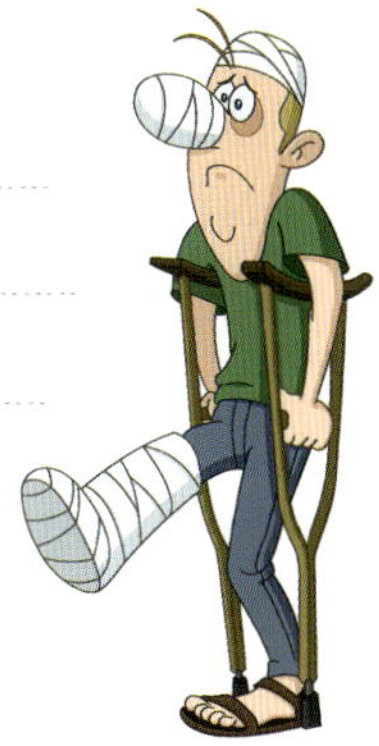

Pair Work

A Complete the sentences with five true statements and five lies.

	Truth or Lie?	O or X
1.	*I haven't cheated* on a test. (cheat)	
2.	______ a competition. (win)	
3.	______ to my parents. (lie)	
4.	______ in the ocean. (swim)	
5.	______ a winning lottery ticket. (buy)	
6.	______ my friend's homework. (copy)	
7.	______ to another country. (travel)	
8.	______ a song from the Internet. (download)	
9.	______ a love letter. (write)	
10.	______ in class. (sleep)	

B Ask your partner to read your sentences. He or she must guess which statements are true or false by writing "O" or "X" in the boxes. How did your partner do?

A I don't think you have traveled to another country.

B You're right!

Wrap-up

A Complete the sentences with the correct forms of the present perfect tense to talk about recent actions.

1. Chen's friend ____________ recently ____________ to Beijing. (move)
2. They ____________ recently ____________ an action movie. (see)
3. I ____________________ to the dentist recently. (not / be)
4. ____________ you ____________ to Janie recently? (talk)
5. What ____________ Yung ____________ doing recently? (be)

B Complete the sentences with the correct forms of the present perfect tense to talk about experiences.

1. ____________ your parents ever ____________ in the Caribbean? (stay)
2. ____________ Mitch ever ____________ golf? (play)
3. Thelma ____________________ biology yet. (not / study)
4. What countries ____________ you ____________? (visit)
5. We ____________________ the Louvre Museum on TV several times. (see)

C Complete the sentences with one of the following phrasal verbs: *go up*, *go back*, *go on*, *go on with*.

1. The hike up the mountain is so tiring Joanne feels she cannot ____________________.
2. The professor was sick. But he ____________________ the lecture anyway.
3. Raphael moved to Bangkok. He has no desire to ____________________ to Mexico.
4. The elevator is broken in Ellen's building, so she has to ____________________ the stairs.

D Look at the pictures. Say what they have already done and what they haven't done yet.

Eric (O)

Petra (X)

Andrew and Marie (X)

Celine (O)

Eric has climbed a mountain.

E Which activities in D have you not done yet? Would you like to do them in the near future?

Unit
8 What would you do?

Warm-up

A Look at the list of amazing abilities. What does each ability mean? Which one do you want to have if you could have one?

B Make your own superhero. What amazing abilities does he or she have? What is your superhero's name?

Heroes		
Name		
Powers		

A Promotion

Conversation

Listen and practice the conversation. 08-01

A What's wrong, Jin?
B I have a problem at work.
A What's the problem?
B I've been offered a new position.
A That's great, isn't it?
B It's in another country. If I accept it, I'll make more money. But I won't see my family or friends very often.
A What will happen if you don't accept it?
B If I don't accept it, they won't offer me a new position for a long time.
A How long do you have to think about it?
B I have to decide by Friday.

Grammar | The First Conditional

A Let's learn about the first conditional tense.

if	Present Simple Tense	will + verb (infinitive)
If	*I wash my car,*	*it will rain.*

If I **see** her tomorrow, I **will tell** her.
If Jim **eats** dinner with Rebecca tonight, he **won't go** out with us.
If they **go** to the party, **will** they **have** a good time?
Will Bobby **be** happy **if** he **gets** a B⁺ in the class?
What **will** she **do if** she **doesn't get** the job?

B Complete the first conditional sentences by matching the correct parts.

1. If I am late for work,
2. If Katrina doesn't like the shirt,
3. Samir will not attend class today
4. Rita and Milo won't like the movie
5. Will Jacob call Amy
6. If Joseph has a good time at the park,

a. if she gives him her phone number?
b. if it snows a lot.
c. if it is really scary.
d. my boss will be angry.
e. he will go back again next week.
f. she will return it to the clothes shop.

Listening

A Listen to the conversations and answer the questions. 08-02

1. What does Karl ask Sandra to do on Friday?
   a. play tennis　　b. have a picnic　　c. see a movie

2. When are Maria and Lionel going to watch the football game?
   a. tomorrow　　b. next Sunday　　c. next Saturday

3. Why didn't Chen finish his report?
   a. The Internet wasn't working.
   b. He didn't have time.
   c. He does not like the class.

B Listen again and choose True or False.

1. Karl and Sandra will watch a movie on Friday if it doesn't rain.
   [True / False]

2. If the Eagles win, Maria will buy dinner for Lionel.
   [True / False]

3. If the teacher gives Chen an extension, he will get an F.
   [True / False]

Making a Story Chain

Listen to the story chain and fill in the blanks in A by using the words in the word box. Then write your own story chain in B. 08-03

will fail　　graduate　　don't　　earn　　lend　　will not

A

A　Can I borrow your book?
B　No, you can't.
A　Why not?
B　If I __________ you my book, I will not read the book. If I don't read the book, I __________ pass the test. If I don't pass the test, I __________ the class. If I fail the class, I will not __________. If I ____ ______ graduate, I will not get a job. If I don't get a job, I will not __________ any money. so that's why I won't lend you my book.

B

A　Can I borrow your ______?
B　No, you can't.
A　Why not?
B　If I . . .

So that's why I won't lend you my ______.

What would you buy?

Conversation

Listen and practice the conversation. 08-04

A What would you do if you won the lottery, Emily?
B I would put the money in the bank.
A The bank? That's boring. Think of an exciting answer.
B Oh, okay. I would buy a car.
A What kind of car?
B A sports car. How about you?
A I would buy a food truck.
B A food truck? What's that?
A It's a truck with a kitchen in the back. I could cook food in the kitchen. Then, I could sell the food to office workers at lunchtime.
B That's a great idea.

Grammar | The Second Conditional

A Let's learn about the second conditional.

if	Past Simple Tense	would + verb (infinitive)
If	*I won the lottery,*	*I would buy a new car.*

If I **saw** a ghost, I **would be** frightened.
If I **had** more free time, I **would go** snowboarding.
Which team **would** you **play** for **if** you **played** professional football?
If you **were** a superhero, which superhero **would** you **be**?
If Rene **didn't have** to work, she **would travel** more often.

B Complete the second conditional sentences by matching the correct parts.

1. How would you earn money
2. If Katie lived in Hawaii,
3. If we didn't have to work on Saturdays,
4. I wouldn't live in this city
5. Would you visit your mother more often
6. If Jamie were a mechanic,

a. she would enjoy the weather more.
b. if she lived near you?
c. if I didn't work here.
d. he would fix his own car.
e. if you lost your job?
f. we would be happier.

Listening

A Listen to the conversation and answer the questions. 08-05

1. What is Zoe's second wish?
   a. $10,000,000.00
   b. a job as a CEO
   c. three more wishes
2. Why does Zoe want to be a CEO?
   a. She wants a big salary.
   b. She wants a big office.
   c. She wants more wishes.
3. What does Zoe's friend think about her third wish?
   a. He likes it. b. He thinks it's unfair. c. He thinks it's smart.

B Listen again and circle the correct words or phrases.

1. If Zoe had ten million dollars, she would buy a huge (house / apartment) in the city.
2. If Zoe had a large office, it would be located on the (bottom / top) floor of the building.
3. If Zoe had one more wish, she would wish for (two / three) more wishes.

TIPS & TIPS Were

If I *were* you, I would . . . (O)   If I *was* you, I would . . . (X)

Pair Work Ask your partner questions in the table. Write their answers in the box.

Interesting Questionnaire		
	Questions	Answers / Reasons
1.	If you were a color, what color would you be?	
2.	If you were an animal, what animal would you be?	
3.	If you were a song, what song would you be?	
4.	If you were a shape, what shape would you be?	
5.	If you were a candy, what candy would you be?	
6.	If you were a movie star, which movie star would you be?	
7.	If you were a fruit, which fruit would you be?	

A If you were a color, what color would you be?
B I would be red.
A Why did you choose red?
B Red is a warm color. And I think I am a warm person.

Muscles use a lot of energy.

Conversation

Listen and practice the conversation. 08-06

A What are you listening to, Matt?
B I'm listening to an audio book.
A What's it about?
B It's about building muscle. If you want to build muscle, you need to eat more calories.
A Why's that?
B Muscles use a lot of energy.
A What about an overweight person?
B When a person has extra fat, he doesn't need a lot of calories. His body can burn the extra fat.
A That makes sense.
B I'm learning a lot about nutrition from this book.

Grammar | The Zero Conditional

A Let's learn about the zero conditional.

if (or when)	Present Simple Tense	Present Simple Tense
If/When	*it rains,*	*the ground gets wet.*

If we heat water to 100 degrees Celsius, it **boils**.
Plants **die if** they don't get enough water and sunlight.
If Randy calls, **tell** him I am at the gym.
When people don't eat healthily and don't exercise, they **don't** usually **live** long lives.
Do people **sleep** better **if** they don't use their phones before bedtime?

B Complete the zero conditional sentences by using the correct forms of the verbs.

1. When it snows, traffic ____________ bad. (be)
2. Ice cream ____________ better if the weather is hot. (taste)
3. Parents worry if their children ____________ home late. (arrive)
4. ____________ people ____________ fat if they eat too much? (get)
5. Dogs ________________________ if you don't scare them. (not / bite)
6. It ____________ if you touch fire. (burn)
7. If you ____________ Adam, tell him I'm in a meeting. (see)
8. What ____________ if you stop going to work? (happen)

Listening

A Listen to the conversation and answer the questions. 08-07

1. What does he ask Isabelle to do if a customer calls?
   a. tell the customer he is in a meeting
   b. tell the customer he is at lunch
   c. tell the customer he is really busy

2. What does he want Isabelle to tell his wife?
   a. that he is in a meeting
   b. that he is at lunch
   c. that he is going to be home late

3. Why is he buying flowers for his wife?
   a. It is their wedding anniversary.
   b. It is her birthday.
   c. He is sorry for working late.

B Listen again and fill in the blanks.

1. If Mr. Parks calls for Mr. Winters, Isabelle should ________________________.
2. If a customer calls for Mr. Winters, Isabelle should ________________________.
3. If Mr. Park's wife calls, Isabelle should ________________________.

Class Activity

Using the zero conditional, write results to the conditions that you think will be the most common answers in the class. Give yourself one point if your answer matches the most common answer in the class.

1.	If people eat too much,	
2.	Babies cry if	
3.	If you put ice in hot water,	
4.	Eileen can't sleep if	
5.	If you see your ex-boyfriend or girlfriend at school or work,	
		Points: ________________

Murphy's Law

Reading

Read the article about Murphy's Law. 08-08

Where Did Murphy's Law Come From?

Have you ever heard of Murphy's Law? Murphy's Law is a humorous law that says, "If something can go wrong, it probably will." For example, imagine you are waiting in line at the supermarket. Your line is going very slowly, so you decide to move to another line. Suddenly, the line you were in before starts moving quickly. And the line you are in now starts moving very slowly. Or imagine you decide to wash your car. You look up, and the sun is shining. You go to the car wash. But on the way home, it begins to rain. These are examples of Murphy's Law. But where does the name come from?

Murphy's Law is named after an American military engineer, Captain Edward Murphy. He was an engineer in the American Air Force in the 1940s. As a project manager, he was responsible for building very complicated machines. Many times, these machines didn't work. Captain Murphy would get frustrated. He would say, "If anything can go wrong with this project, it will." His team members liked this expression. They called it "Murphy's Law." Eventually, Murphy's Law became a popular expression in the United States and around the world. Today, we use the expression to describe an unlucky situation. It is funny how a common expression such as Murphy's Law started a long time ago with just one person. He got frustrated when things didn't work, just like we do today.

Comprehension Check Answer the questions about the article.

1. What is Murphy's Law?
2. What is an example of Murphy's Law?
3. Who is Murphy's Law named after?
4. When was Edward Murphy an engineer in the Air Force?
5. Why did Edward Murphy become frustrated?

Speaking

Complete the sentences below with examples of Murphy's Law.

1. If you see a handsome man in your class, *he will have a girlfriend.*
2. If you wear white pants to a restaurant . . .
3. If you forget your umbrella at home . . .
4. If you wash your car . . .
5. If you see a shirt you really like at a shop . . .
6. If your phone isn't working and you go to the service center . . .

Pair Work

Match the conditions with the pictures. Then ask your partner questions by using conditionals. Cross out the pictures after you have used them.

a. If it rains . . .
b. If you wake up early . . .
c. If you get rich . . .
d. If you drink too much coffee . . .
e. If it is sunny . . .
f. If you are late . . .
g. If it snows a lot . . .
h. If you eat too much . . .
i. If it is very hot . . .

A What will you do if it is sunny?
B If it's sunny, I will play golf.

Writing

Write a short essay about what you would do if you won $1,000,000.

If I won a million dollars, I would . . .

Wrap-up

A Complete the first conditional sentences.

1. If it rains, Betty ________________ to work. (drive)
2. If Andrew ________________ to class today, Jun will bring him his homework. (not / come)
3. ____________ they ____________ at a good restaurant if they go downtown? (eat)
4. What ____________ the teacher ____________ if the students are bored? (do)
5. Jenny will call her friend tonight if she ____________ time. (have)

B Complete the second conditional sentences.

1. Which superhero ____________ you ____________ if you were a superhero? (be)
2. Would you move to China if you ____________ a new job? (get)
3. If Anthony ____________ the lottery, he would buy a new apartment. (win)
4. Samantha and Alexandra would go shopping on Fridays if they ________________ work. (not / have to work)
5. If our house were bigger, my brother and I ________________ a bedroom. (not / share)

C Complete the zero conditional sentences.

1. If you touch a hot stove, it ____________ your hand. (burn)
2. If it snows too much, schools ____________ classes. (cancel)
3. Dogs ________________ if they are well trained. (not / bite)
4. ____________ plants ____________ if there isn't enough rain? (grow)
5. People ________________ it when their friends lie to them. (not / like)

D Answer these silly second conditional questions with your own information.

1. If you went back in time to the past, what year would you go back to?
2. If you found $1,000,000 in a suitcase, what would you do?
3. If you were a country, what country would you be?
4. If you were able to change your appearance, what would you change?
5. If you were the president of your country, what would you do?

E Say about a time when you have experienced Murphy's Law.

Unit 9 Innovators

Warm-up

A Look at the pictures. Who are these famous inventors? Put the numbers in the correct places.

1. Benjamin Franklin 2. Marie Curie 3. Leonardo da Vinci 4. Alexander Graham Bell 5. Thomas Edison

B Do you know who invented the item(s) in the pictures? Put the correct inventor's name in each blank.

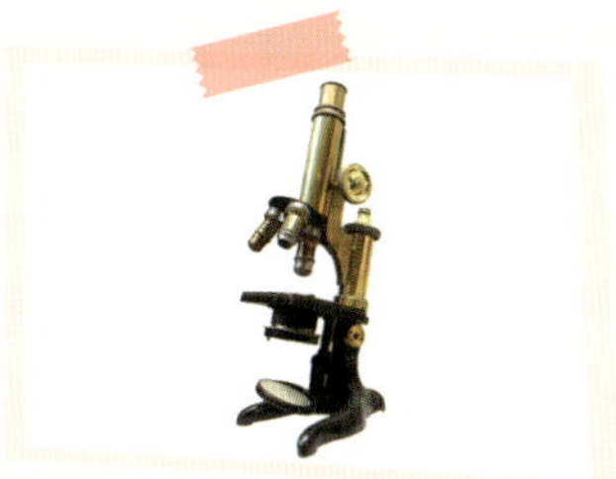

1. ____________________

2. ____________________

3. ____________________

4. ____________________

5. ____________________

Who was it invented by?

Conversation

Listen and practice the conversation. 09-01

A Tabatha, do you know who invented the Tesla electric car?
B No, I don't, Jahid.
A It was invented by Elon Musk. He's a Canadian inventor and billionaire.
B How did he become so rich?
A He helped create PayPal in the 1990s.
B Wow. I didn't know that. What else has he invented?
A The Falcon rocket was invented by him.
B What does the Falcon rocket do?
A It sends important items to astronauts in space.
B No way. That's awesome!

Grammar | Passive Voice 1

A Let's learn about the past simple passive voice.

Present Simple Passive Voice Subject + am/is/are + Past Participle + (by)	Past Simple Passive Voice Subject + was/were + Past Participle + (by)
The laundry **is done by** Maria on Tuesdays. Snails **are eaten by** people in France. The dish is called escargot.	The Tesla **was invented** by Elon Musk. Who **was** *The Lord of the Rings* **written by**? **Was** the robber **seen by** anybody?

B Rewrite the sentences in the passive voice.

1. Thieves sometimes steal cars in my neighborhood.
   → ______________________________
2. John ate the sandwiches for the party.
   → ______________________________
3. Sal didn't see the driver that hit him.
   → ______________________________
4. Edison invented the light bulb.
   → ______________________________
5. Tornadoes cause a lot of damage.
   → ______________________________

Listening

A Listen to the lecture and choose the correct words. 09-02

1. Who is Shepard Fairey?
   a. a street artist　　b. a sculptor　　c. a musician

2. Why did Shepard Fairey become famous?
   a. He made a sculpture of Barack Obama.
   b. He designed a building for Barack Obama.
   c. He made a painting of Barack Obama.

3. What does Jeff Koons do?
   a. takes care of animals　　b. makes sculptures　　c. paints buildings

B Listen again and choose True or False.

1. Street artists paint on the walls of buildings and on bridges. [True / False]
2. Jeff Koons creates sculptures of small balloon animals. [True / False]
3. Jeff Koons' sculpture of a giant balloon dog was purchased for $58.4 million. [True / False]

Pair Work

A Ask your partner who the following items were invented by. Use the past simple passive voice.

Thomas Edison

Steve Jobs

Erno Rubik

George Crum

Percy Spencer

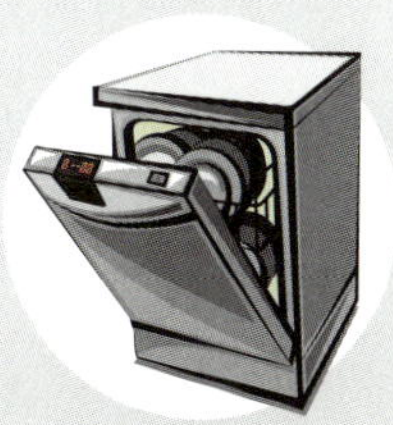
Josephine Cochrane

Guglielmo Marconi

Karl Benz

John Montagu, 4th Earl of Sandwich

(your choice)

A　Who was the light bulb invented by?
B　It was invented by Thomas Edison.

B Which of the inventions do you think is most useful in your life?

My Favorite Book

Conversation

Listen and practice the conversation. 09-03

A Have you read *For Whom the Bell Tolls*?
B No, I haven't.
A It's my favorite book. It was written by Ernest Hemingway. He's my favorite author.
B It is kind of old, isn't it?
A Yes, but it's great.
B I don't like reading very much. I like watching movies. Have you seen *The Lord of the Rings*?
A No, I haven't.
B It was directed by Peter Jackson. He's a great director from New Zealand.
A Oh, I didn't know that. I read the book though. It was written by J.R.R. Tolkien.
B Really? Maybe I'll read that one.

Vocabulary | Interesting Jobs

A Guess what the person in each picture does.

inventor

author/novelist

graphic designer

app developer

sculptor

art gallery curator

animator / cartoonist

street artist

B Match the jobs with the correct descriptions.

1. ____________ a person who writes books
2. ____________ a person who draws characters for comic strips or television
3. ____________ a person who chooses art for a gallery
4. ____________ a person who creates images for books, TV, movies, the Internet, etc.
5. ____________ a person who creates new products
6. ____________ a person who makes sculptures
7. ____________ a person who develops apps
8. ____________ a person who paints large pictures on walls by using spray paint

Listening

A Listen to the conversation. Then complete the information in the stolen car report. 09-04

Police Report

Car Type

Color Year

Location of Crime

B Listen again and choose the correct words.

1. The woman's car was stolen this (morning / afternoon).
2. The thief was (seen / not seen) by the woman.
3. Her car was parked in the (supermarket / clothes shop) parking lot.

C Listen to a follow-up conversation. Then choose True or False.

1. The officer has some good news for Ms. Parker. [True / False]
2. The officer didn't find the person who stole Ms. Parker's car. [True / False]
3. Her car was found three blocks from the supermarket. [True / False]
4. The woman must sign some documents at the police station. [True / False]
5. The woman will go to the police station in one hour. [True / False]

Pair Work

A Imagine a thief has broken into your home. Use the picture clues to ask and answer questions with your partner about what was stolen.

A What was stolen?
B Some cash was stolen.

B Ask your partner if he or she has ever had anything stolen? What was stolen? When did it happen?

A Have you ever had anything stolen?
B Yes, I have. My bag was stolen two years ago.

Solar Energy

Conversation

Listen and practice the conversation. 09-05

A Elsie, I read an interesting article today about solar energy.
B What's the article about, Seth?
A More German homes are powered by solar energy than in any other country.
B Really?
A That's right.
B Does Germany make the most solar panels, too?
A No, it doesn't. More solar panels are made in China than in any other country.
B That makes sense.
A But many of those solar panels are sold to other countries like Germany.
B Oh, I see.

Grammar | Passive Voice 2

A Let's learn about the passive voice with various prepositions.

be pleased about / at / with	be concerned about / with	be amazed at
be surprised at / by / with	be famous for	be interested in
be covered in / with	be made of / from	be scared of
be tired of	be related to / with	be filled with

The mountaintop **is covered with** snow.
Mr. Kim **was surprised by** the news.
Lots of people **are scared of** spiders.
Some students **are interested in** studying abroad.

B Complete the sentences with the correct prepositions.

1. We are pleased ______________ your decision.
2. They were tired ______________ instant noodles.
3. Jessica was surprised ______________ the sudden question.
4. Many countries are concerned ______________ environmental problems.
5. The dress is made ______________ expensive silk.

Listening

A Listen to the conversations and answer the questions. 09-06

1. How many drivers use the George Washington Bridge each day?
   a. fewer than a million
   b. a million
   c. more than a million

2. What kind of meat is expensive in Thailand?
   a. chicken
   b. beef
   c. pork
3. What type of team doesn't the school have?
   a. men's basketball
   b. women's basketball
   c. women's volleyball

B Listen again and choose True or False.

1. More lanes are needed on the George Washington Bridge. [True / False]
2. Apples and pears are tropical fruits eaten in Thailand. [True / False]
3. Men's and women's volleyball games are played in the gym. [True / False]

Pair Work Use the table to make a quiz. Then ask your partner the quiz questions. Who was the winner? Don't show the answers to your partner.

Quiz Questions	Answer Key	Your Partner's Answers
Name the currency that is used in ____________ (country).		
Name three foods that are eaten in ____________ (country).		
Name a language that is spoken by people from ____________ (country).		
Name a song that is sung by ____________ (famous singer).		
Name a movie that is directed by ____________ (famous movie director).		
		Score: ___ / 5

A Name the currency that is used in Britain.
B The British pound is used in Britain.

I am my own boss.

Reading

Read the interview. 09-07

New Tab New Tab

Work.com

By Julia Winters

This week, I am interviewing Kyle Reynolds, a graphic designer. We sat down for a nice conversation in his studio at his apartment in Chicago, Illinois.

JW *Thanks for talking to me today, Kyle.*

KR My pleasure, Julia.

JW *So tell me about your job.*

KR I'm a graphic designer. I design logos, signs, and other images for companies here in Chicago. And I'm a freelancer. So I am my own boss.

JW *How do you fill your days?*

KR My days are filled doing projects for different companies. For example, right now I'm working on an interesting project. I'm designing a logo for a new software company. They asked me to design three logos. Then, they'll choose their favorite one.

JW *How many hours do you work in a day?*

KR When I'm busy, I work 8 to 10 hours a day. But when I'm not busy, I work 4 or 5 hours a day.

JW *How do you get paid?*

KR I get paid for each project. That's the downside of freelance work. If I don't work, I don't get paid. So I always try to have at least one or two projects going.

JW *What about vacations?*

KR Since I don't work for a company, I'm not given any paid vacation time. But I try to give myself one week off every winter. It's cold in Chicago in winter, so it's important for me to go somewhere warm.

JW *Do you like your job?*

KR When a project is finished and the customer is happy with it, I feel very satisfied.

JW *Thanks again for talking to me today.*

KR You're welcome.

Work.com

Comprehension Check Answer the questions about the interview.

1. What does Kyle do as a graphic designer?
2. What project is Kyle working on right now?
3. How many hours per day does Kyle work when he is not busy?
4. What is the downside of freelance work?
5. How much vacation time does Kyle take each year?

Writing

Write a short essay about your job. What do you spend most of your time at work doing?

Group Work Every group member chooses a picture from the table. Then describe the object to the group members by using the passive voice.

Wrap-up

A **Rewrite the sentences in the passive voice.**

1. Peter moved the table into the kitchen.
   → ______________________________________

2. His daughter doesn't play the clarinet.
   → ______________________________________

3. Do the students listen to classical music?
   → ______________________________________

4. Elon Musk invented the Tesla sports car.
   → ______________________________________

5. The flood caused a lot of damage.
   → ______________________________________

B **Look at the pictures. What items were stolen by the thieves?**

1. 

2. 

3. 

4. 

C **Complete the sentences with the correct prepositions.**

1. This restaurant is famous ____________ fresh seafood.
2. Maria is really scared ____________ snakes.
3. Many visitors were very pleased ____________ the festival.
4. You will be amazed ____________ the cost of this bag.
5. His book is filled ____________ wonderful stories.

D **Describe the items by using the passive voice.**

1. 

2. 

3. 

4. 

Unit 10

Gadgets and Technology

Warm-up

A Say the names of the items in the picture. Which items are examples of new technology? Which ones are examples of old technology?

B Which items do you use daily? Which items do you use occasionally or not at all? Write the answers in the table.

Daily	Occasionally or Not at All

New Phone

Conversation

Listen and practice the conversation. 10-01

A Jin, how long have you had your phone?
B I've only had it for a few months.
A It's nice. Is it expensive?
B It's a little expensive. I have to pay $65.00 per month for two years.
A $65.00! That's a lot. I pay $30.00 per month.
B How long have you had your phone?
A Two and a half years.
B Are you going to buy a new one?
A I'm thinking about it. But I'm looking for something cheaper than yours.
B Let's go to Tech Mart. It has lots of options.

Grammar | Present Perfect

A Let's learn about the present perfect tense.

have/has + Past Participle & for / since	
How long **have** you **lived** in New York? - I have lived here **for** ten years. How long **have** Jane's parents **lived** in their house? - They have lived in their house **for** seventeen years.	How long **has** Adele **been** a professional singer? - She has been a professional singer **since** 2008. How long **hasn't** Jim **played** tennis? - He hasn't played tennis **since** he hurt his elbow.

Fred moved to New York ten years ago. → Fred has lived in New York for ten years. → **Fred lives in New York now.**

B Complete the questions with the present perfect tense. Complete the answers by using *for* or *since*.

1. A How long ____________ the Petersons ____________ in this city? (live)
   B They have lived in this city ____________ seven years.
2. A How long ____________ Vera ____________ her best friend? (know)
   B She has known her best friend ____________ 2009.
3. A How long ____________ the students ____________ English? (study)
   B They have studied English ____________ five years.
4. A How long ____________ the car ____________ broken down? (be)
   B It has been broken down ____________ last week.

Listening

A Listen to the conversation and answer the questions. 10-02

1. What's wrong with the speakers' television?
   a. The sound system is broken.
   b. The picture quality is not good.
   c. The screen is too small.

2. How long have the speakers had the television?
   a. They have had it for eight years.
   b. They have had it since 2008.
   c. They have had it for a short time.

3. Where are they going to go this weekend?
   a. Tech Mart b. Super Mart c. TV Mart

B Listen again and choose True or False.

1. The speakers are going to fix the television. [True / False]
2. The speakers bought the television in 2008. [True / False]
3. The speakers went shopping for a new TV last weekend. [True / False]
4. The man wants to buy a bigger television. [True / False]

Group Work Do a survey of your group members to see who has done each of these the longest.

How long have you . . . ?	Period of Time	Student's Name
(have) your phone		
(live) in your neighborhood		
(play) your favorite sport		
(have) the bag or backpack you are using now		
(drive) a car		
(have) your computer		
(know) your best friend		
(study) English		

Jack has had his phone for three years. He has had his phone the longest.

I lived in Paris for two years.

Conversation

Listen and practice the conversation. 10-03

A Your country is really beautiful, Phuong.
B Thank you. How long have you lived in Vietnam?
A I've lived here for two months now.
B Where did you live before you moved here?
A I lived in Paris.
B How long did you live in Paris?
A I lived there for two years. I was a student.
B What did you study?
A I studied filmmaking at the Paris Film Institute. I'm making a movie here in Hanoi.
B Wow, cool!

Grammar | Past Simple and Present Perfect

A Let's study the differences between the past simple tense and the present perfect tense.

Past Simple	Present Perfect
How long **did** you **live** in Paris? – I **lived** in Paris for two years. How long **was** Anthony a teacher? – He **was** a teacher for thirty years. They **didn't study** French for a long time.	How long **have** you **lived** in Hanoi? – I **have lived** in Hanoi for two years. How long **has** Alice **been** an engineer? – She **has been** an engineer for twenty-two years. We **haven't studied** math for a long time.

B Complete the sentences with the past simple or present perfect tense.

1. Bob ____________ in Tokyo for ten years. He is going to move to Kobe next year. (live)
2. Maria ____________ an accountant for ten years. She is retired now. (be)
3. A How long ____________ you ____________ golf? (play)
   B I have played golf for five years.
4. Eric and Theresa ____________ for six months. They broke up yesterday. (date)
5. Tim ____________ Russian for four months. He is studying Russian right now. (study)
6. I ____________ meat for many years. I'm a vegetarian now. (eat)
7. Saydee and Carolyn ____________ to school together for several years. They are now in the same 5th grade class. (go)
8. Sandy's parents ____________ married for twenty years. Tomorrow is their anniversary. (be)

Listening

A Listen to the conversations and answer the questions. 10-04

1. How long has Francis been engaged?
   a. three months　　b. three weeks　　c. three years
2. How long has Erica been dating Tom?
   a. three months　　b. six months　　c. nine months
3. How long has Stephanie been married?
   a. two years　　b. five years　　c. ten years

B Listen again and choose the correct words.

1. Francis asked Bethany to marry him (in a park / at a restaurant).
2. Erica had a crush on Tom for (months / weeks).
3. Richard (has been / was) married for two years.

Vocabulary | Romance Words and Expressions

A Let's learn the dating words and expressions.

be married

date / see someone

be engaged

be divorced

break up with / split up with someone

ask someone out

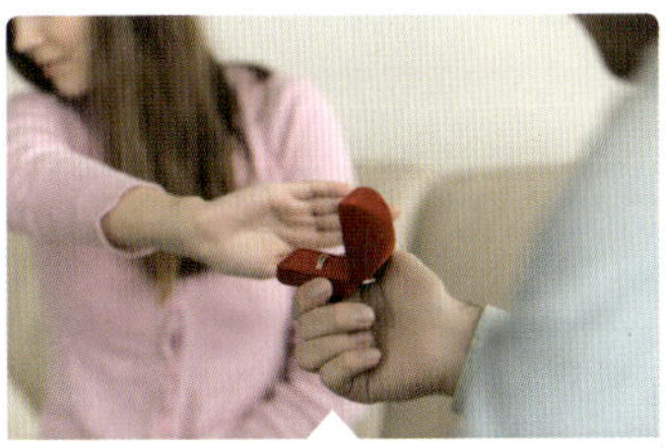
reject / turn down someone

have a crush on someone

use an online dating site

B Ask a classmate questions by using the dating words and expressions in the pictures.

A Have you used an online dating site?
B Yes, I have. I met my girlfriend online.

I had already bought this one.

Conversation

Listen and practice the conversation. 10-05

A Nice tablet, Finn. Is it new?
B Yes, it is, Marta. I bought it about a week ago.
A You don't look too happy about it.
B I'm not very happy.
A Why is that?
B I bought it from a shop in my neighborhood for $400.00.
A That's not a bad deal.
B I know. But right after I bought this one, my friend Janet asked me if I wanted to buy her tablet for $50.00.
A What did you do?
B Nothing. I had already bought this one when she called.

Grammar | Past Perfect

A Let's learn about the past perfect tense.

had + Past Participle
My parents **had** already **left** when I came home. Steven **had** already **eaten** when his friend invited him to dinner. Youmi **hadn't sung** in front of people before she joined the school's music club. **Had** John **studied** French before he moved to Paris? What **had** Shelly **known** about the job before she accepted it?

My parents had already left when I came home.

My parents left. (before another action in the past)	*I came home.* (an action in the past)	Now

B Complete the sentences with the past perfect tense.

1. When Don called, Susan ____________ already ____________ her phone. (turn off)
2. Shinzo ____________ Spanish before he moved to Spain. (study)
3. Where ____________ they ____________ before they came to the meeting? (go)
4. ____________ he ____________ basketball before he joined the team? (play)
5. My friend ____________ already ____________ for work when I called to ask her for a ride. (leave)

Listening

A Listen to the conversation and choose the correct words. 10-06

1. Carol Freeman ordered (Internet / phone) service from the company.
2. The woman (has / hasn't) received Internet service from the company.
3. The technician will go (tomorrow / next week).

B Listen again and choose True or False.

1. The technician went to the woman's house at 11:00 a.m. [True / False]
2. The woman had been home when the technician came. [True / False]
3. The technician will go again at 10:00 a.m. [True / False]

Timeline

What have you done today? Complete the timeline below. Then read them out loud by using the past perfect tense.

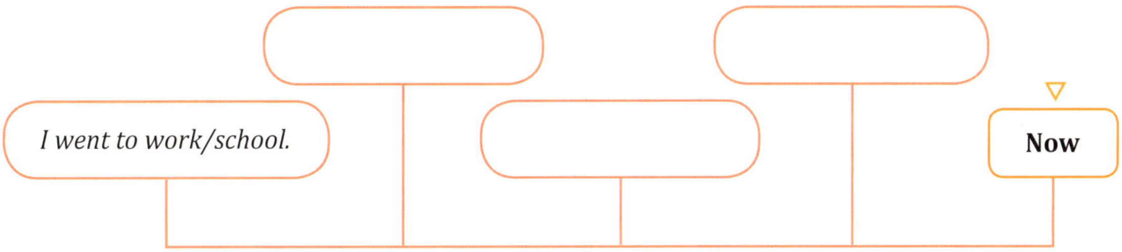

I had gone to work before I called my sister.

Pair Work

Imagine that your partner has just used the expressions in the left column. Then ask your partner why he or she used the expressions. Write your partner's reasons in the right column.

Why did you say . . . ?	Before I said that,
"I'm sorry."	*I had stepped on someone's foot.*
"I'm tired."	
"It hurts!"	
"I'm happy."	
"Oh, no!"	
"No, thank you."	

Video Games and the Future of Gaming

Reading

A Read the article. 10-07

Tech Weekly Feb 15

The Future for Gamers

In the 1990s, video game players, or "gamers," enjoyed playing video games on Nintendo or Sony PlayStation game consoles. However, game consoles have changed a lot since the 1990s. New game consoles, such as the X-Box, Nintendo Wii, and PlayStation 3, allow users to connect to the Internet. So gamers can play together with people from all over the world. Some gamers prefer to play video games only on their computers. In this case, they don't need a game console. They just need game software that can be downloaded onto their PC or laptop.

Different kinds of games have become popular, too. For example, first-person shooter (FPS) games have larger worlds and more levels. New gamers enjoy playing FPS games because they are more difficult. With all of the changes that have occurred since video games became popular, it is not hard to imagine that things will change in the future. One of the newest game technologies is virtual reality (VR). With VR, you don't need a television screen or monitor. The screen is inside a pair of virtual reality glasses. With the glasses on, gamers can see 360 degrees. Gamers feel like they are inside the world of the game. VR technology has become less expensive since it was invented. Soon, it will be a part of every gamer's life.

Comprehension Check Answer the questions about the article.

1. What game consoles did gamers enjoy playing in the 1990s?
2. How have game consoles changed over the past 20 years?
3. What kind of game has become popular with new gamers?
4. How do gamers play games on their PCs?
5. How does a person use VR technology?
6. How has the price changed for VR technology?

B Have you ever tried VR technology? If yes, what was it like? Share your answer with the class.

Your Most Important Possession

Writing

Write an essay about your most important possession. What is it? How long have you had it? Where did you get it? Why do you like it? It doesn't have to be expensive. It can have sentimental value, too.

Group Work

Make groups of three to five people. Share your essay with the group members. Complete the table with your group members' answers.

Name	Item	Why It Is Important

This tablet is my most important possession. My parents bought it for me. I like it because I can use it to chat with my friends and surf the Internet.

Pair Work

Choose an item you have with you right now. Make a true or false sentence about how long you have had that item. Let your classmates see the item. Then ask your classmates to decide if you are telling the truth or lying.

A I have had this wallet for ten years.
B It doesn't look very old. I think you are lying.
A Yes, I'm lying. I have had this wallet for three years.

Wrap-up

A Complete the sentences with *for* or *since*.

1. Elena has had her watch ____________ four years.
2. Penelope and Martin have known each other ____________ high school.
3. Where has Doug been ____________ the past ten years?
4. I haven't listened to this CD ____________ 2015.
5. Has she played the piano ____________ university?

B Complete the sentences with the past simple or present perfect tense.

1. Jules and Veronica ____________ friends for years. They are friends now. (be)
2. The movie ____________ in the theater for months. It's not in the theater anymore. (be)
3. They ____________ their father for a week. But their father is coming home tomorrow. (see)
4. Chang ____________ at the same company for twenty years. He's retired now. (work)
5. Pierre and his wife ________________________ for almost five years. Next week is their 5th anniversary. (marry)

C Use the timeline to make true sentences about Marcus' day.

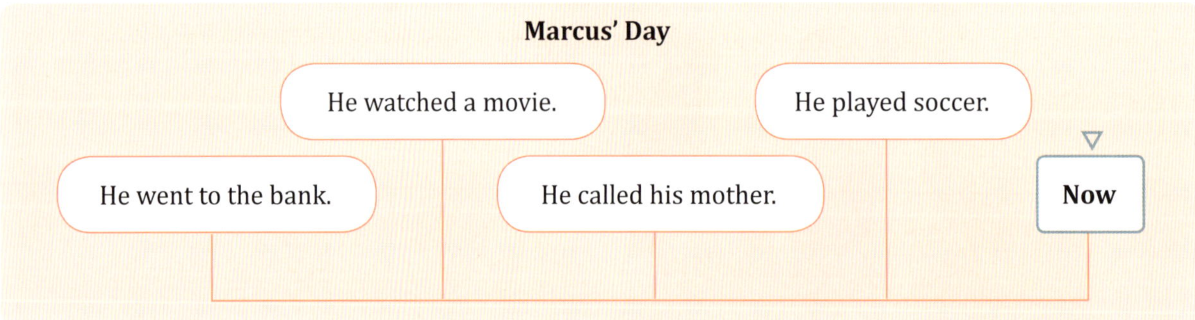

Marcus had called his mother before he played soccer.

D Do you have these items below? Say how long you have had them.

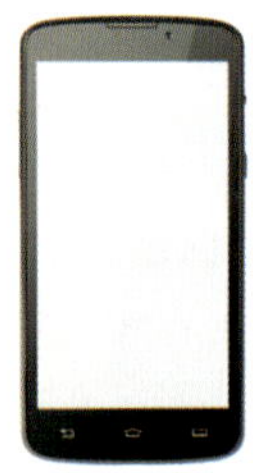

E Do you like video games or smartphone games? Describe your favorite game. Then say why you like it.

Unit 11

I'm Stressed!

Warm-up

A Look at the pictures. Why could these events be stressful? Which one would be the most stressful for you?

a big speech

an important game or match

learning to drive

a snoring spouse

an important test

a job interview

B What kinds of stressful events do you experience in your life? Write some examples in the box.

Stressful Events

C What makes you feel the most stressed in your life?

My job makes me feel the most stressed. I give a lot of important presentations. I feel nervous before each presentation. It gives me a lot of stress!

I'll help you.

Conversation

Listen and practice the conversation. 11-01

A What's wrong, Fran?
B I have a big presentation on Friday. I'm really nervous about it.
A I'll help you prepare for it.
B You will?
A Why don't we meet in the library at 5:00 this evening?
B I'm meeting my professor at 5:30. How about 6:00?
A Sure. There's a projector in the library's meeting room.
B Do you think it's going to be available then?
A Definitely. No one ever uses that room.
B Great. I'm going to go home and practice now. I'll see you at 6:00!

Grammar | Future

A Let's learn about the future tenses.

Present Simple (scheduled events)	**Present Continuous** (arrangements with someone)
The train **leaves** at four o'clock. Ted's plane **doesn't arrive** until after twelve o'clock in the morning. **Does** the class **start** on Friday?	Jacob **is meeting** his parents tonight for dinner. Yui **isn't giving** Nancy a ride to the airport. **Are** Lydia and Paul **having** coffee together this weekend?
will + verb (promises, predictions, offers, and decisions)	**be going to + verb** (plans and intentions)
I'll help you. Jennifer **won't get** the job. **Will** Mr. and Mrs. Miller **have** fun in Norway this summer?	Young **is going to** travel to the USA this year. Fernando **isn't going to** teach English in Korea after university. **Is** Ming **going to** visit his uncle this winter?

B Complete the sentences with the present simple or present continuous tense.

1. The bus ____________ at 7:00 a.m. tomorrow. (leave)
2. ____________ the bank ____________ at 10:30 a.m. on Monday? (open)
3. Maxine ________________________ tennis with us this weekend. (not / play)

C Complete the sentences with *will + verb* or *be going to*.

1. It's hot in here! I ________________________ the window. (open)
2. Marcia ________________________ the chess match. (not / win)
3. Sam ________________________ in finance after university. (work)

Listening

A Listen and complete the talk. 11-02

Hi, Janine. This is Cynthia. I need to talk to you. I have ______________________ tomorrow, but I'm so scared. The interview is for ______________________ at Freemont Industries. This is my dream job. I don't know ______________________. I don't know ______________________. I'm kind of freaking out. The interview is with the sales director. I'm meeting him ______________________ at 11:00 a.m. I've worked so hard for this job. I really think ______________________. But I can't relax. Please call me when you get this message.

B Listen to the rest of the talk. Then choose True or False.

1. The company's sales director is going to interview Cynthia tomorrow. [True / False]
2. Cynthia is not very worried about the interview. [True / False]
3. Cynthia is going to wear black pants, a white blouse, and a blue jacket. [True / False]
4. Janine thinks Cynthia will get the job. [True / False]
5. Cynthia feels better after talking to Janine. [True / False]

Pair Work

A Find the correct sets of problems and offers. Then complete the table.

It's hot in here. I'll get some. I'll give you a ride. This box is too small.
I need to go to the airport. I can't hear the music. We are out of milk. I'll help you.
I'll open the window. It's too heavy. I'll turn it up. I'll get you a bigger one.

	Problems	Offers
1.		
2.		
3.		
4.		
5.		
6.		

B Tell your partner some problems. Then have your partner offer help.

I have an important test on Friday. I am so nervous and worried . . .

The Honeymoon

Conversation

Listen and practice the conversation. 11-03

A Johnny, where are you and Jessica going to go on your honeymoon?

B We're going to go to Hawaii.

A Nice!

B I'm a little stressed. I don't know if Jessica's going to like my surprise.

A What's the surprise?

B We're taking surfing lessons with a professional surf instructor.

A Cool. She'll love it.

B Do you think so?

A Absolutely. She's very athletic.

B I'm sure we'll have a great time.

Class Activity

A Imagine a friend is visiting your group from another country. The friend is going to stay for the weekend. Make plans for him or her. Where is your group going to take the friend? What are you all going to do?

Plan a Weekend Trip in Your City		
	Saturday	**Sunday**
Morning		
Afternoon		
Evening		

B Now share your group's weekend plans with other groups. Which group's plans are the most exciting? Ask your teacher to choose a winner from your class.

Listening

A Listen to the conversation and choose the correct answers. 11-04

1. What holiday is mentioned in the conversation?
   a. Christmas b. Halloween c. Thanksgiving

2. What is the woman's new year's resolution?
   a. She will read lots of books.
   b. She will quit drinking alcohol.
   c. She will quit smoking.

3. How many books will the man read in a year?
   a. 25 b. 50 c. 52

B Listen again and choose True or False.

1. The woman had a great birthday. [True / False]
2. The woman is worried she won't be able to keep her new year's resolution. [True / False]
3. The man doesn't think he will be able to keep his new year's resolution. [True / False]

Class Activity

A A new year's resolution is a promise people make to themselves on January 1. As a class, make a list of popular new year's resolutions in your country. Write the list in the box.

New Year's Resolutions

B Choose your new year's resolution for next year. Then ask three classmates about their new year's resolutions and how they plan to keep them. Write their answers in the table.

Name	New Year's Resolution	How will he/she keep it?
David	He will quit drinking coffee.	*He will drink tea instead.*

I'll be living in Canada.

Conversation

Listen and practice the conversation. 11-05

A Are you worried?
B No, not really.
A You should be.
B Why?
A This time next year, you will be living in Canada.
B I'm excited.
A Think about it. There won't be any of the foods you like there.
B Of course there will be. I'm moving to Vancouver. It's an international city.
A It won't be the same.
B I hope it isn't the same. I want a new experience.

Grammar | Future Continuous

A Let's learn about the future continuous tense.

will + be + -ing
Stevie **will be singing** at the stadium next week. *The Great Game* **won't be playing** in movie theaters next month. **Will** Erin **be waiting** for Shinzo when he comes back? What **will** she **be doing** ten years later?

B Complete the sentences with the future continuous tense.

1. Jeff and his brother ____________ on the team this time next year. (play)
2. ________ he ________ on Friday at seven o'clock? (study)
3. Harry ____________ the class on Friday. (not / attend)
4. ________ Jules and James ____________ their anniversary next Monday? (celebrate)
5. Where ________ she ________ to school next year? (go)
6. What ________ the students ________ a year after graduation? (do)
7. Yui and Chen ____________ married sometime next year. (get)
8. Henry ____________ his parents next weekend. He's going to be too busy. (not / call)

Listening

A Listen to the conversation and choose the correct answers. 11-06

1. What does the man think humans will be driving in 30 years?
   a. flying cars　　b. electric cars　　c. gasoline-powered cars
2. What do the men think people will be eating in 30 years?
   a. organic food　　b. processed food　　c. fast-food
3. What clothes do the men think people will be wearing in 30 years?
   a. People will be wearing space clothes.
   b. People will be wearing the same clothes as now.
   c. They don't know.

B Listen again and choose True or False.

1. The men are talking about things that happened 30 years ago. [True / False]
2. Both men agree about the kind of food people will be eating in 30 years. [True / False]
3. Both men have great style in clothes. [True / False]

In the Year 2050

A Look at the Venn diagram. Say what activities people are doing these days. Then make predictions about the activities people will be doing in 2050. What activities do you think will be the same in the future as they are today?

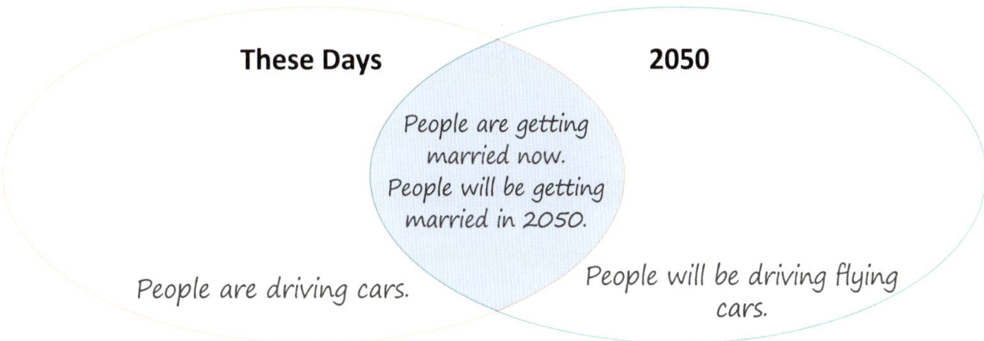

B Now make a Venn diagram for yourself. What are you doing these days? What do you think you will be doing in 2050? What activities do you think will be the same?

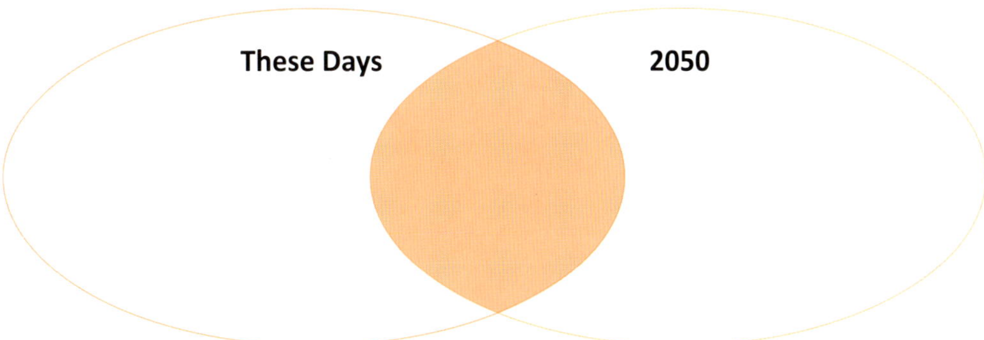

A Record Deal

Reading

A Read the interview with the singer. 11-07

The Music Journal | July 25

Up and Comers

Jonathan Miller, Columnist

Indie rock group Dirt Spoon is based in Brooklyn, New York. They have recently signed their first record deal. I talked to the lead singer, Simon Pilgrim, about his band's new album and their recent success. We also discussed their concert this Friday at the New York Convention Center. I think we're going to be seeing a lot more of these guys in the future.

Jonathan *Simon, it must be exciting to sign a record deal.*

Simon Yes, it is. We have worked really hard to get to this point.

Jonathan *How long has your band been together?*

Simon We have been together for five years now. And we will continue to be a band for a long time, too.

Jonathan *Some bands fight with each other. This can happen when a band becomes popular. The band members start arguing. Do you get along with your band mates?*

Simon We really like each other. We rarely argue. And when we argue, we don't yell at each other.

Jonathan *That's great. So you have a concert this Friday at the New York Convention Center. Is that right?*

Simon Yes, we are going to play for over 10,000 people. It will be our biggest show ever.

Jonathan *That's great. Are you nervous?*

Simon I think we are all a little nervous. This show is very important.

Jonathan *What do you think your band will be doing ten years from now?*

Simon Ten years from now, we will be selling out shows for 50,000 people or more!

Jonathan *Wow, that's very ambitious. Thanks for talking to me today.*

Simon Sure. My pleasure.

Comprehension Check Answer the questions about the interview.

1. Where do the members of the band live?
2. When is their next concert?
3. How long has the band been together?
4. How many people are they going to play for on Friday?
5. What does Simon Pilgrim think the band will be doing ten years from now?

B Do you have any ambitious goals or dreams for the future? Say what they are.

Writing

A Look at the music posters below. What kind of show do you think each poster is advertising?

B Now write a short promotional article for your own show. Include information like the place, date, and time.

Dirt Spoon will be performing this Friday at the New York Convention Center. Dirt Spoon is an amazing rock band. The lead singer's name is Simon Pilgrim. The show is going to start at . . .

Class Activity

Find someone who is going to do the following activities this weekend. If your classmate answers yes, write his or her name in the table.

	Are you going to . . . this weekend?	Name
1.	go out of town	
2.	eat at a nice restaurant	
3.	meet a high school friend	
4.	see a movie	
5.	go to a nightclub	
6.	sleep in until noon	
7.	do homework / office work	
8.	do housework	

Wrap-up

A Complete the sentences with the present simple or present continuous tense.

1. The train always ________ at 9:00 a.m. (arrive)
2. ________ the post office ________ at 9:00 a.m. on weekdays? (open)
3. My father ________ me to dinner tomorrow night. (take)
4. Mario ________ us in front of the movie theater this evening. (not / meet)

B Complete the sentences with *will* or *be going to*.

1. It's cold in here! I ____________ the door. (close)
2. I think Anthony ____________ the job. (get)
3. ________ you ____________ your friend this weekend? (visit)
4. Yumi ____________ for a job at a bank after college. (apply)

C Complete the sentences with the future continuous tense.

1. April and Sam ____________ lunch at this time tomorrow. (eat)
2. ________ Hong ____________ French in Paris at this time next year? (study)
3. Henry ____________ in the dormitory next semester. (not / live)
4. ________ she ____________ her birthday next Sunday? (celebrate)
5. Which countries ________ they ____________ in next year? (travel)

D What will the people be doing at this time next year? Use the picture clues.

Fred will be working in an office at this time next year.

E Find a promotional article or advertisement for an event in an online newspaper or magazine. What is it for? Who may be interested in it?

Unit 12 Big Life Changes

Warm-up

A Who said what? Put the letters in the correct places.

a. I started university. b. We bought a house. c. I moved to a new city.
d. We had a baby. e. I started a new job.

B Think of three big life changes you have experienced. Write them in the table below. Were they positive or negative experiences?

My Big Life Changes		
1.		Positive / Negative
2.		Positive / Negative
3.		Positive / Negative

Driving in a New City

Conversation

Listen and practice the conversation. 12-01

A Rush hour traffic in Bangkok is really terrible.
B I know. There are too many cars on the roads.
A Watch out! That motorcyclist is driving really dangerously.
B I see him.
A He shouldn't be driving so fast on a rainy day.
B Now it's raining really hard.
A Do you have an umbrella?
B Yes, I do. It's in the back seat.
A Found it! Uh, oh, there's only one.
B I guess we'll have to share it.

Grammar | Adverb 1

A Let's learn about adverbs of manner.

adjective + ly / ily	Irregular Adverbs
Carlos walks too **slowly**. Elizabeth speaks **quickly**. We didn't paint the house **properly**. Why are the neighbors speaking so **loudly**? Joy **angrily** yelled at her little brother. Frank **noisily** entered the apartment, waking his whole family.	Cyrus runs **fast**. It rains **hard** in Bangkok during the rainy season. Why does Paul wake up **early**? Jack doesn't play golf **well**.

B Complete the sentences with the correct adverbs.

1. The basketball team ____________ celebrated their win. (excited)
2. Why did Samantha answer the teacher's question so ____________? (rude)
3. Winnie doesn't speak ____________ enough. I can't hear her. (loud)
4. Does Youngmi speak English ____________? (good)
5. Jamie's parents live ____________ in the country. (happy)
6. The team is playing ____________. I think they will win. (hard)
7. Rita is sitting ____________ in the chair. (comfortable)
8. The city is too polluted to see the clouds ____________. (clear)

Listening

A Listen to the conversations and answer the questions. 12-02

1. What city have the man and the woman recently moved to?
   a. Bangkok b. Manila c. Seoul
2. Why does the mother think the baby is crying?
   a. The baby is hungry. b. The baby is sleepy. c. The baby is sick.
3. What kind of apartment did the company give the man and the woman?
   a. a small apartment b. an old apartment c. a big apartment

B Listen again and choose True or False.

1. The man thinks he and the woman can learn the streets of the city more easily together. [True / False]
2. The woman was not sleeping very well. [True / False]
3. The couple thinks Thai people have treated them unkindly. [True / False]

Pair Work

Interview your partner by using the questions in the table. Your partner should answer by using adverbs of manner.

Adverbs of Manner Questionnaire	
How do you . . . ?	**Partner's Answers**
usually sleep	*I usually sleep peacefully.*
normally drive	
frequently work	
usually study	
normally eat	

Describing Actions

Describe how these people do the following actions. Use the pictures and words.

drive / angry

sleep / peaceful

eat / healthy

run / fast

He drives angrily.

Our New House

Conversation

Listen and practice the conversation. 12-03

A Let's move indoors so I can show you the inside of the house.
B That sounds great.
A Follow me downstairs. Now this is the family room.
B It's so big.
A This area is great if you have children. Now let's go upstairs. I'd like to show you the bedrooms.
B Wow. I love the wallpaper in this bedroom.
A This wallpaper is everywhere in the house. It's really expensive.
B What's over here?
A This is the dining room. And that's the kitchen. Please feel free to look around.
B Oh, I love this house. Let's buy it!

Grammar | Adverb 2

A Let's learn about adverbs of place and time.

indoors outdoors upstairs downstairs everywhere nowhere around	yesterday tomorrow today now later last week last year
The children played **indoors** because it was raining. Rebecca is going **upstairs** to get her phone from her bedroom. Yuki and Daniel danced **around** the dance floor for hours.	Jane called her brother **yesterday**. I'll call you **tomorrow**. Where did your parents go on vacation **last year**? Sujin didn't eat breakfast **today**. School was canceled **last week**.

B Complete the sentences with the correct adverbs of place from above.

1. Zack takes his dog ______________ he goes. He even brings his dog into the classroom.
2. Fran used to live ______________ in the basement of the building, but now she lives on the 5th floor.
3. The dog isn't allowed to come ______________. It sleeps outside.
4. William's parents like to barbecue in the summer. They even eat ______________ on the patio.
5. We looked ______________ for the keys, but we could not find them.

C Complete the timeline with the correct adverbs of time from above.

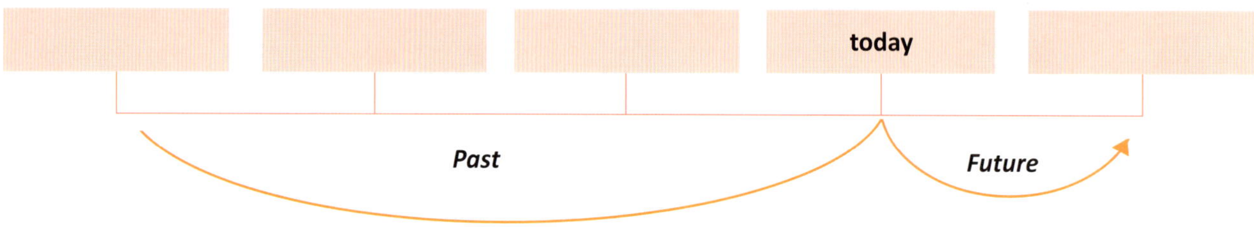

Listening

A Listen to the conversation and choose the correct words. 12-04

1. The couple is (moving out / moving in).
2. The woman wrote (letters / words) on the boxes.
3. The boxes for the upstairs are too (heavy / big) for the woman to carry.
4. The box with the letter "O" on it is for the (outdoors / office).

B Listen again and choose True or False.

1. The box with the letters "L" and "R" is for the living room. [True / False]
2. The woman forgets what the letter "O" is for. [True / False]
3. The man's office is upstairs. [True / False]

Speaking

Describe what the people in the picture are doing by using adverbs.

A person is sleeping upstairs in a bedroom.

Pair Work

A With your partner, make a list of activities that can be done indoors. Then make a list of activities that can be done outdoors. Share your lists with the class.

Indoors	Outdoors
People can watch television indoors.	*People can have picnics outdoors.*

B Use the adverbs of time below to write five true sentences about yourself in the table.

Today	*I visited my parents today.*
Tomorrow	
Yesterday	
Last Week	
Last Year	

You'll Get Over It

Conversation

Listen and practice the conversation. 12-05

A Mom, this was a huge mistake! I want to get on a plane and come home.
B You're just homesick, Carly. You'll get over it soon enough.
A I don't think so.
B You just need to get out of the dorm room and meet some other students.
A I know. I'm trying hard to meet people, but I'm shy.
B Are there any clubs on the campus that you could join?
A There's a piano club. But I have to audition to get in.
B There you go! You're a great piano player. I'm sure you'll get in.
A Do you think so?
B Once you make some friends, your semester in England will go by so quickly.

Grammar | *Get*

A Let's learn about phrasal verbs with get.

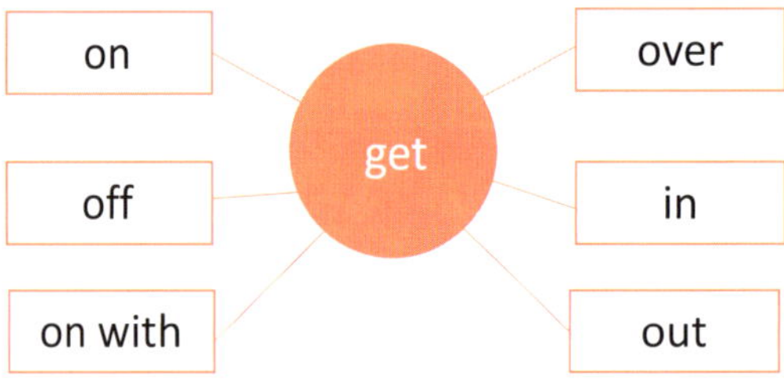

Get on the bus!
Please **get off** the roller coaster carefully.
Never mind that noise. Let's **get on with** the class.
Julie has been crying for weeks. She can't **get over** breaking up with her boyfriend.
I'll give you a ride to work. **Get in**.
Let's **get out** of the taxi here. We can walk the rest of the way.

B Complete the sentences with the correct phrasal verb.

1. I have to ____________ the train. It's leaving soon.
2. Break time's over. Let's ____________ work.
3. The bus is too full. I can't ____________.
4. Please ____________ my bike. It's too small. You're going to break it!
5. It was hard for the basketball team to ____________ losing the championship game.
6. Children need to ____________ of the house more. They're too lazy these days.

Listening

A Listen to the conversation and answer the questions. 12-06

1. How's the weather in Delhi?

   a. cool　　b. –10 degrees Celsius　　c. hot

2. What is the man's job at the textile factory?

   a. executive　　b. HR manager　　c. sales manager

3. How does the man feel about the food in the city?

   a. It's too spicy.　　b. It's incredible.　　c. It's terrible.

B Listen again and choose the correct words.

1. The woman lives in (Delhi / Minnesota).
2. The man's company supplies textiles to more than (200 / 300) companies.
3. The company has taken the man to (lunch / dinner) a few times.
4. The man (has / hasn't) spent much time walking around the city.

Class Activity

A Write your answers in the table.

Something you can . . .	My Answer	Points
get off	*I can get off a bus.*	
get in		
get on		
get out of		
get over		
get on with		
		Total: ___ / 6 points

B Compare your answers with your partner's answers. If an answer matches your partner's answer, give yourself a point. The pair with the most points in the class wins.

Tim's Tiny House

Reading

A Read the article about Tim. 12-07

Tim's Tiny House Blog

"Conservation is a state of harmony between men and land."

– Aldo Leopold

Welcome to the Tim's Tiny House Blog! I'm Tim, the owner of a tiny house in the mountains of Colorado, USA. I have lived in a tiny house since 2009, and I love it. Before I built my tiny house, I had lived in a big house in the city of Denver, Colorado. My big house was expensive. Heating in the winter and air conditioning in the summer cost me a lot of money. I

also had a lot of stuff. Too much stuff! Then, I heard about the tiny house movement. I learned that lots of people around the world were building tiny houses. These people wanted to help the environment by using less energy and by taking up less space. They wanted to live more cheaply, too. I sold my house and most of my things. Then, I bought some land in the mountains about one hour away from the city of Denver. I designed and built my tiny house, which is only the size of a bedroom in most normal houses. There are a tiny kitchen, a little living room, and a small bathroom with a shower. I sleep in the small loft upstairs. I installed solar panels, so my lights and my electronic items can be powered by the sun. My only monthly bill is for my telephone and Internet service. Life goes by more slowly in the mountains. And I like that. Life in the city was too fast. If you are interested in the tiny house movement, email me at timstinyhouse@bloglife.com.

Comprehension Check Answer the questions about the article.

1. How long has Tim lived in a tiny house?
2. Why was Tim's big house expensive?
3. How does the tiny house movement help the environment?
4. How does Tim power his electronic items?
5. What bills does Tim have to pay each month?

B Would you be interested in living in a tiny house? Why or why not?

Listening

A Listen to the woman's talk. Then put the pictures in the correct order from 1 to 4. 12-08

☐

☐

☐

☐

B Are any of these pictures true for your life? Do you recycle? Are you a vegetarian? Do you have solar panels or an electric car?

Writing

What are some things you already do to improve the environment? What more could you do to help?

Class Activity

A Make a group of 5 or 6 students. Take turns reading your essays. Make a larger list of things you can do to improve the environment.

Ways to Improve the Environment	
1.	
2.	
3.	
4.	
5.	

B Share your list with the other groups in the class. What were the most popular answers?

Wrap-up

A Complete the sentences with the correct adverbs.

1. The audience clapped ____________ when the amazing piano concert ended. (loud)
2. Why do you speak so ____________, Amanda? I can't hear you. (soft)
3. Werner kicks the ball ____________ when he plays soccer. (hard)
4. Do Jason and Emile play billiards ____________? (good)
5. My aunt sings ____________. She's a professional opera singer. (beautiful)

B Complete the sentences with the adverbs *around*, *downstairs*, *everywhere*, *indoors*, *outdoors*, and *upstairs*.

1. If we move ____________, you can see my new kitchen. It's really beautiful.
2. Joe looked ____________ the house for his keys for thirty minutes before he found them.
3. Yunghwan's parents' bedroom is ____________ on the 3rd floor. Her bedroom is on the second floor. And her sister lives ____________ in the basement. They have a really big house!
4. My father does not like going ____________. He prefers to stay home and to watch TV.
5. Tuesday was a public holiday, so there were children ____________ at the amusement park.

C Complete the sentences with the phrasal verbs *get in*, *get on*, *get on with*, *get out, get over*, and *get off*.

1. Let's ____________ the swimming pool. The water looks really nice.
2. Halftime is over. Now it's time to ____________ the second half of the football match.
3. Please ____________ my skateboard. I'm afraid you are going to hurt yourself.
4. Don't ____________ of the car until I have completely stopped.
5. Please ____________ the scale. I need to know how many kilograms you weigh.
6. One year later, the runner was still sad he lost the race in the Olympics. He just couldn't ____________ it.

D Imagine you wanted to build a tiny house. Where would you build it? What do you think your life would be like?

E Have you ever volunteered? If yes, where did you go, and what did you do? If you answered no, are you interested in volunteering?

Answer Key

Unit 1 **These Days**

Warm-up p. 11

1. Peter Harris
2. Amy Holiday
3. Kate Tripper
4. Mary Ellen
5. Emily Jackson
6. Dave Winston

It's nice to see you again.

Grammar p. 12

B

1. doesn't have
2. went
3. traveled
4. exercise
5. brushes
6. didn't see
7. practice
8. go

Listening p. 13

Script

A: Hey, Yoshi.
B: Hi, Tisa.
A: How are your classes going this semester?
B: Not bad. I like my chemistry class. But I really hate my writing class. It's so boring. How about you?
A: I like my schedule. I don't start class until after twelve o'clock. But my chemistry class is really difficult. Maybe you can help me study.
B: Sure. I'd be happy to.
A: Thanks.

A

1. c
2. a
3. a

B

1. True
2. False
3. False

Pair Work p. 13

A

1. What is your name?
2. What is your job?
3. What do you do during the week?
4. What do you do on the weekend?
5. How was your break?
6. Where did you go?
7. What did you do?
8. How long did you stay there?

I was just watching TV.

Grammar p. 14

B

1. is watching
2. was sleeping
3. is studying
4. was taking
5. was driving
6. is raining
7. was, doing
8. Are, eating
9. wasn't snowing
10. are driving

Listening p. 15

Script

1. A: What were you doing at 11:00 a.m. on Saturday, Neil?
   B: I was watching a hockey game. My son is on the team. His team usually plays games on the weekend.
2. A: What were you doing at 9:00 this morning, Devon?
   B: I was working. I was talking to a customer on the phone when my boss gave me a lot of files.
3. A: What were you doing when I called you this morning? Were you playing video games, Byron?
   B: Yes.
   A: I told you no more video games. You need a job.
   B: Okay, you're right.

A

1. Devon
2. Byron
3. Neil

B

1. Saturday
2. his customer
3. playing video games

What do you want to do?

Vocabulary p. 16

A

1. do judo
2. drink in a bar
3. bake a cake
4. sing karaoke
5. play video games
6. practice the trumpet

Listening p. 17

Script

A: I can't believe it's Friday. The week went by really fast.
B: I know. What do you want to do this weekend?
A: Well, we usually drink and sing karaoke, but I want to do something different.
B: Sure. Do you have any ideas?
A: I don't want to stay inside and play computer games or board games. Why don't we play tennis?
B: Good idea. There's a tennis court near my house.
A: Okay, let's go!

A

1, 2, 4, 5, 6

B

1. False
2. False
3. True
4. True

My Job Routine

Reading p. 18

Comprehension Check

1. He usually eats in the company cafeteria.
2. Because he likes to sleep longer.
3. She puts them on her blog.
4. Makayla's hobby is the same as her job.
5. She doesn't like the hours.

Listening p. 19

Script

Hi. I'm Lars. I'm 27, and my life isn't very stressful. I live with my parents, so I don't pay any rent. My mother asked me to look for a job in the newspaper, but those jobs don't look very fun. Some people say I am lazy, but I think I'm smart. Going to work every day to a boring job sounds stupid to me.

Hello. I'm Jean. I own my own bakery. My bakery is small, so I do all the work: baking, making coffee, and answering the phone. My husband says I work too much, but I love it. I don't think you can work too much if you love your job.

I'm Milan. I am really stressed. In my office, people always give me more work. I can't take it. I want to quit. But I can't quit because I need the money.

A

1. b	2. a	3. a
4. a	5. c	6. a

B

1. 27, stressful
2. owns, bakery
3. stressed, wants

Wrap-up p. 20

A

1. played	2. didn't eat	3. do
4. study	5. travels	6. went

B

1. was sleeping	2. is driving
3. weren't, working	4. Is, smoking
5. was, doing	6. Is, studying

Unit 2 Then and Now

There used to be a school here.

Grammar p. 22

B

1. used to play	2. didn't use to come
3. didn't use to have	4. did, use to go
5. used to believe	6. did, use to dislike
7. used to be	8. did, use to go

Listening p. 23

Script

I used to be in a soccer club when I was eleven. My friends and I loved soccer. We used to play every Saturday morning. Our team was called the Tigers. This is us. From the left side, this is Joseph. He used to be really fast. So he was a midfielder. Next to Joseph is Christy. She was our defender. She used to be good at stopping the other team. Webb was short, but he used to be able to kick the ball very hard. So he was the striker. Victoria used to catch the ball really well. She was our goalkeeper. And next to Victoria is my little brother, Pete. He joined the team after me. He used to copy everything I did. The last one on the right side is me. I used to like scoring goals. So I played forward. Boy, do I miss the Tigers and those days!

A

B

1. False	2. False	3. True
4. True	5. False	

My Hometown

Listening p. 25

Script

A: I like your house. When did you move in?
B: I moved in about three years ago.
A: Oh, wow. What did your old house look like?
B: It was small. It wasn't big like this house. But I liked the color. That's why I painted my new house yellow, too.

A: I'm sure your old house was very nice.
B: It was a nice house. But it didn't have a garage, and I wanted to park my car inside during the winter.
A: Now you have a nice garage.
B: I know. It's very convenient in the winter.

A

1. b 2. c

B

1. c 2. a 3. c
4. b

Now I'm used to living alone.

Grammar p. 26

B

1. is used to getting
2. isn't used to having
3. Is, used to driving
4. are used to eating
5. are, used to doing
6. aren't used to practicing

My neighborhood is very different.

Reading p. 28

Comprehension Check

1. He used to live in a quiet neighborhood.
2. He lives in the city. / He lives in an apartment.
3. They used to play in the park.
4. They play inside.
5. He used to drive.
6. He takes the subway.

Listening p. 29

Script

1. Hey. I'm Simone. I used to check my text messages all the time. I probably spent five or six hours a day on my phone. My husband used to get really angry. Now I only use my phone for 30 minutes a day. And my life is much better.
2. Hi. I'm Jezebel. I started smoking when I was 16 years old. My friends did it, so I did it too. I used to smoke one pack per day. I know. That's really bad. But I quit six months ago, and I feel great.
3. Hey, everyone. My name is Adelaide. I love coffee. I used to drink like five cups a day. Sometimes six! Unfortunately, I still drink coffee. But now I drink only one cup of coffee per day. And I drink it in the morning.

A

1. bad habits 2. husband 3. started
4. changed

B

1. b - f - j 2. c - d - k 3. a - f - l

Wrap-up p. 30

A

1. used to live
2. didn't use to exercise
3. did, use to eat, used to eat
4. did, use to go, used to go

B

1. isn't used to working
2. is used to having
3. Are, used to driving
4. aren't used to living
5. are, used to playing

Unit 3 People I Know

Whose watch is this?

Vocabulary p. 32

B

1. intelligent 2. charming 3. artistic
4. rude 5. curious

Grammar p. 33

B

1. Whose 2. Who's 3. Who's
4. whose 5. Who's

Is this yours?

Grammar p. 34

B

1. hers 2. mine 3. ours
4. his 5. theirs 6. yours

Listening p. 35

Script

1. A: Listen, everybody! Whose jacket is this? It's red, and it looks expensive.
   B: Where's Jacob? I think it's his.
2. A: Excuse me, everyone! But does anyone know whose phone this is? It's silver, and it has a brown case.
   B: Oh, you found it! It's mine. Thank you!
3. A: Turn off the music, please! There's a green SUV outside with the lights turned on.
   B: Isn't that yours, Judith?

4. A: Excuse me, but did anyone lose a purse? I found it behind the sofa.
B: Where's Emily? She was looking for her purse ten minutes ago. I think it's hers.

A

mine, hers, yours, his

B

1. b 2. b 3. b
4. c

I'm really excited!

Grammar p. 36

B

1. annoying 2. disappointing 3. shocked

C.

1. confusing 2. excited
3. frightening, frightened 4. interested, boring
5. confusing, confused

Listening p. 37

Script

A: I'm bored. Let's watch that new documentary about jazz music.
B: No, thanks. I'm not really interested in that.
A: There's an interesting art exhibit at the museum. Why don't we go there?
B: I saw it two weeks ago.
A: Oh. We can see the new action movie. Brad Cochrane is in it. It looks exciting.
B: I don't like his movies. He's annoying.
A: Then what do you want to do?
B: Let's play video games. Space Fighter II is amazing.
A: Okay. I guess we can do that.

Script

A: I'm hungry. Let's go to a restaurant.
B: Where do you want to go?
A: How about the Italian restaurant near here?
B: No way. I ate there last week. The food was disgusting.
A: Okay. How about the Mexican restaurant?
B: It's too dark inside. It's kind of depressing.
A: Where do you want to go?
B: Let's go to the diner. It's far from here, but I am excited to try the new menu there.
A: Okay. Let's go!

B

1. b 2. b 3. b

My BFF

Reading p. 38

Comprehension Check

1. It means "joy."
2. She's kind, sensitive, and funny.
3. She wants to be a veterinarian.
4. They're from India.
5. She's tall and has black hair and big eyes.
6. Because Farah visited Anna when she was sick.

Wrap-up p. 40

A

1. Whose 2. Who's 3. Whose
4. Whose 5. Who's

B

1. his 2. mine 3. hers
4. theirs 5. ours 6. yours

D

1. confused 2. frightening 3. boring
4. interesting

Unit 4 Different Cultures

Meet My parents

Listening p. 43

Script

A: Tell me a funny story about living abroad.
B: I used to work in an office in Thailand. I was at the office one day, and I was a little tired. So I took off my shoes and put my feet up on my desk. Then, my boss came into my office and got really angry. In Thailand, it's rude to point your feet at someone.
C: I took my girlfriend to meet my Chinese grandmother. My grandmother is a great cook, and she made my favorite noodles for us. I told my girlfriend to eat the noodles really loudly. Making noise while eating is polite in China. My girlfriend was really noisy. My grandmother was so happy!
D: In France, it's polite to kiss people hello. When I introduced my sister to a Frenchman, he kissed her. She was really embarrassed.

A

1. b 2. c 3. a

B

1. a 2. c 3. b

You have to use two hands.

Grammar p. 44

B

1. must / has to
2. must / has to
3. Do, have to
4. don't have to
5. must / have to
6. Do, have to

Listening p. 45

Script

What do I have to do today? Hmm, let me see. I had better write this down:

First, I must finish my chemistry report. It is due on Friday at noon.

Second, I have to buy pasta, tomato sauce, and bread at the grocery store. I'm making dinner for Emil and Fran this evening. I should probably buy a bottle of wine, too.

Third, I have to pay my rent. It's due today.

Last, I should call my mother. It's her birthday tomorrow.

A

To Do List

Must / Have to . . .

1. finish my chemistry report
2. buy pasta, tomato sauce, and bread
3. pay my rent

Should

4. call my mother

B

1. False
2. True
3. False
4. False

Rules are rules.

Grammar p. 46

B

1. You must not smoke here.
2. You must not use your cell phone here.
3. You must not speak here.
4. You must not eat or drink here.

A Year of Teaching Abroad

Reading p. 48

Comprehension Check

1. He thinks they're really polite.
2. The language is very difficult.
3. Receiving things with two hands, and bowing.
4. Because too much eye contact is rude in Japan.

Wrap-up p. 50

A

bow, wave, handshake, *wai*

B

1. must / have to
2. doesn't have to
3. don't have to
4. must / has to
5. must / has to

C.

1. You must not drink alcohol. / You mustn't drink alcohol.
2. You must not take a picture. / You mustn't take a picture.

Unit 5 A Slice of Life

Do you want to play kick volleyball?

Grammar p. 52

B

1. into
2. outside
3. down
4. up
5. toward
6. over

Listening p. 53

Script

A: Do you want to play Snakes and Ladders?

B: What's that?

A: It's a board game. It's really fun.

B: How do you play?

A: You place your game piece on the first square. Then, you roll the die and move your game piece up the board. The first person to reach the 100th square wins.

B: Is that all?

A: Not quite. When you land on a ladder, you can move your game piece up the ladder toward the 100th square.

B: That's good.

A: It is. But watch out! When you land on a snake, you have to move your game piece down toward the first square.

B: Oh, no!

A

1. b
2. b
3. b
4. b

B

1. False
2. True
3. False

Listening p. 53

Script

Move right one square. Move down two squares. Move right three squares. Move down one square. Go across the bridge. Move up two squares. Move right one square and into the house. What color house are you in?

. . .

That's right. The blue house!

It's organic!

Grammar p. 54

B

1. losing 2. to call 3. to go
4. to watch 5. living 6. to eat

Listening p. 55

Script

Welcome to *Maddie's Life*, a weekly podcast. I'm your host, Madison Chan, and today I'm going to share three things I love about the summer with you.

Number one: I love drinking a cold glass of homemade lemonade on a hot summer day. For a great lemonade recipe, visit my blog. I love to share great recipes with my fans!

Number two: I enjoy sunbathing at the beach with my BFF Elizabeth. It's so much fun to lie in the sun. But don't forget to wear sunscreen. You have to protect yourself from the sun!

Number three: I really love eating a vanilla ice cream cone on a hot summer day. For a list of the best shops to buy vanilla ice cream cones in Los Angeles, visit my blog.

Thanks for listening. Bye!

A

1. c 2. a 3. c

B

1. True 2. True 3. False

I'm afraid of flying.

Vocabulary p. 56

A

1. heights 2. spiders
3. flying 4. small spaces
5. snakes 6. water
7. mice 8. going to the dentist
9. public speaking

Listening p. 57

Script

A: What do you have a fear of, Harim?

B: I have a fear of dogs.

A: Why are you afraid of dogs?

B: When I was young, there was a big, scary black dog in my neighborhood. It used to bark at me really loudly on my way home from school. One day, it bit me on the leg. After that, I became really afraid of dogs.

A: What happens when you see a dog?

B: I start shaking, and my heart beats really fast.

A: What's the most difficult thing about your phobia?

B: It's really difficult when I visit friends and family with dogs. When I go to their houses, they have to put their dogs in another room.

A: Do you think you will overcome your fear someday?

B: Yes. I don't think I will ever have a big dog as a pet. But I might have a small dog as a pet.

A

1. a 2. b 3. c

B

1. False 2. True 3. True
4. False

Grow some herbs!

Reading p. 58

Comprehension Check

1. Because they take up a small amount of space.
2. basil and thyme
3. You should make mint tea.
4. Water the herbs often, give them lots of sunlight, and rotate the herbs toward the sun.
5. So they look better and taste better.

Wrap-up p. 60

A

1. into 2. over 3. outside
4. toward

B

1. a. Do they enjoy dancing?
2. b. Sharon wants me to call her tonight.
3. b. I would like Aaron to stop playing video games now.
4. a. Paul likes jogging with his friends.

C

1. She is afraid of flying.
2. She wants to go to the Philippines.
3. Her heart beat fast, she started sweating, and she couldn't breathe.

Unit 6 Famous People

Look! There he is.

Grammar p. 62

B

1. taller
2. more exciting
3. funnier
4. wetter

C

1. shortest
2. worst
3. politest
4. hottest

D

2. is shorter than her brother
3. is richer than Jerome
4. is poorer than Jeremy
5. is fatter than Janine
6. is healthier than Georgia

I need to memorize this.

Vocabulary p. 64

A

1. film director
2. drummer
3. the cast
4. orchestra
5. ballerina
6. audience
7. musician
8. conductor

Listening p. 65

Script

A: That was amazing!
B: I know. The violinist Ming Chao was incredible.
A: She's only 22 years old. But she's the best in the world.
B: That's for sure. What about the conductor? He's old, but he's more energetic than people much younger than him.
A: He's from Italy. He's very famous.
B: Really? What's his name?
A: His name is Antonio Ferrara. He's 88 years old. But he's not the oldest conductor in the world.
B: Are you serious?
A: There's a 92-year-old conductor from Germany. He travels the world conducting orchestras all year round.
B: Wow. I guess working hard keeps you young.
A: Yeah. I guess so.

A

1. b
2. c
3. a

B

1. False
2. True
3. True

Pair Work p. 65

A

1. the Blue Diamond
2. the Pacific Ocean
3. Tokyo
4. the cheetah
5. the blue whale
6. Delhi, India
7. (Answers will vary.)

Famous Families

Listening p. 66

Script

1. A: I think Will Smith's family is the most talented family in Hollywood.
 B: Really? Why do you think so?
 A: Everyone in his family acts in movies or makes music.
 B: I didn't know that.
 A: Will and Jaden even acted together in a sci-fi movie.
2. A: Do you know who the Hemsworth brothers are?
 B: Sure. Chris and Liam are in really successful action movies.
 A: Did you know they have another brother?
 B: No, I didn't.
 A: His name is Luke. He's shorter than Chris and Liam. But he stars in one of the most popular television series on TV.
3. A: Do you know who the Olson twins are?
 B: No, I don't.
 A: They were child actors in the 1980s and 90s. But now they are entrepreneurs.
 B: What do they sell?
 A: They sell cosmetics, clothes, and jewelry. They're very rich!

Listening p. 66

Script

The Jacksons were a family of successful singers from Gary, Indiana. In the 1960s, the oldest sons in the family formed a group called the Jackson Five. The Jackson Five became very popular in the 1970s and sold lots of records. Michael Jackson was the most famous group member. In the 1980s, Michael Jackson had a wonderful career as a solo artist. His album *Thriller* sold millions of copies worldwide and made Michael Jackson an international superstar. Unfortunately, Michael Jackson died on June 25, 2009. He was 50 years old.

A

worldwide, oldest, album, popular, solo artist

B

1. a
2. b
3. c

Listing p. 67

Script

A: What do you think about Katy Perry and Lady Gaga, Kevin?
B: I think they're good singers. But I think Taylor Swift is better.
A: What about fashion? Who is the most fashionable?
B: Lady Gaga wears some really amazing dresses. I think she is the most fashionable.
A: Not me. Her dresses are too strange. I think Katy Perry is the most fashionable. Who is the most talented musician?
B: Well, that's definitely Taylor Swift.
A: Why do you say that?
B: She writes her own music. And she plays the piano better than all of them.
A: Really?
B: Yeah. She's also the tallest.
A: I thought Katy Perry was the tallest.
B: Nope. Taylor Swift is 178cm tall. She is five centimeters taller than Katie Perry.

A

1. b 2. c 3. b

B

1. False 2. True 3. False
4. False

The Hollywood Walk of Fame

Reading p. 68

Comprehension Check

1. They love movies.
2. Bars and restaurants were near their hotel.
3. They went to Hollywood Boulevard.
4. They went on a star maps tour.
5. She thought it was more beautiful than Britney Spears' house.

Wrap-up p. 70

A

1. bigger 2. more exciting 3. friendlier
4. politer

B

1. smartest 2. most exciting 3. most polluted
4. funniest

Unit 7 Accidents

Warm-up p. 71

A

1. A snake bit my finger.
2. Oh, no! I hit that car.
3. Ouch! A bee stung me.
4. My ankle really hurts.
5. I cut my finger.
6. I hurt my leg playing soccer.

Where are you?

Grammar p. 72

B

1. has, had 2. have bought
3. Have, been 4. has, eaten
5. hasn't seen 6. have visited
7. have, drunk 8. has, played

Listening p. 73

Script

A: Oh, no! What have you done?
B: I've hurt my foot
A: How?
B: Barbara and I have recently become interested in outdoor activities. So we decided to take mountain climbing lessons.
A: And?
B: We went to a park. They taught us how to climb up and down a rock wall. The wall was six meters tall.
A: Then what happened?
B: Barbara went up and down the wall just fine. The teacher was very impressed.
A: Barbara is very athletic.
B: I know. But I'm clumsy. I climbed up the wall all right. But when I was coming down, I fell on my right foot and broke it.
A: Oh, no!
B: The doctor hasn't told me how long I have to wear the cast.
A: I'm sure it's going to be at least a month.

A

1. b 2. a 3. c

B

1. True 2. True 3. False

I've been in a car accident.

Grammar p. 74

B

1. has, been 2. has, eaten
3. haven't traveled 4. Have, studied
5. has, listened 6. Have, visited
7. have lived 8. has, dated

Listening p. 75

Script

A: Has a dog ever bitten you?

B: Yes. When I was young, my cousin's dog bit me.

A: A dog has never bitten me. But a snake has.

B: A snake! How did that happen?

A: I was hiking with my father. And I stepped on a water snake. It bit me on the leg.

B: Did you go to the hospital?

A: No. Water snakes are not poisonous. My father helped me. And we finished the hike.

B: Wow. You're strong.

A: Thanks. Have you ever broken a bone?

B: No, I haven't. How about you?

A: Yes. I was hiking, and I tripped on a rock. I fell and broke my arm.

B: You've had a lot of accidents hiking.

A: I know.

A

1. hasn't 2. has 3. has

B

1. b 2. c 3. b

Can't we go back?

Grammar p. 76

B

1. go up 2. go on with 3. go back
4. go on

Ouch! I cut my finger.

Listening p. 77

Script

A: What are you doing?

B: I'm chopping some carrots. I'm making chicken soup.

A: Yum!

B: Ouch! I've cut my finger. It's bleeding.

A: Here. Use this towel. Put pressure on it.

B: Thanks.

A: Is it bad?

B: I don't know. I can't look. You look.

A: Okay, let me see it. Hmm. It's not a deep cut. But you'll need a bandage. Let me get one.

B: Thank you.

A: Here it is. Let me put it on.

B: That's better.

A

1. carrots 2. finger 3. towel
4. man

Script

A: I've never cut myself while cooking. I don't know what happened.

B: I'm sorry I bothered you.

A: I need to be more careful.

B: Why don't you sit down? I'll finish the soup.

A: Then I'll tell you how to make it. And you do the cutting and cooking.

B: Great idea. Are you sure you're okay?

A: Yeah. It hurts a bit. But I think I'll be fine.

B: Okay. So what do I need to do?

A: Finish cutting those carrots. And be careful!

B: Thanks.

B

1. False 2. True 3. True
4. False

Look at my car!

Reading p. 78

Comprehension Check

1. She woke up late.
2. She was looking down at the spilled coffee.
3. She was in the back car.
4. He was really angry.
5. It was Matilda's fault.

Wrap-up p. 80

A

1. has, moved 2. have, seen 3. haven't been
4. Have, talked 5. has, been

B

1. Have, stayed 2. Has, played 3. hasn't studied
4. have, visited 5. have seen

C

1. go on 2. went on with 3. go back
4. go up

Unit 8 What would you do?

A Promotion

Grammar p. 82

B

1. d 2. f 3. b
4. c 5. a 6. e

Listening p. 83

Script

1. A: Hello?

   B: Hey, Sandra. This is Karl. Do you want to play tennis on Friday?

   A: Sure. But I heard it might rain on Friday.

   B: If it doesn't rain, we'll play tennis. If it rains, we'll see a movie.

   A: That sounds great!

2. A: Hello?

   B: Hey, Lionel. This is Maria. Do you want to watch the football game at my house next Sunday?

   A: I'd love to. The Eagles are definitely going to win.

   B: No way! The Tigers are much better than the Eagles.

   A: Do you want to make a bet?

   B: Sure. If the Eagles win, I'll buy you dinner.

   A: Okay. And if the Tigers win, I'll buy you dinner.

   B: Deal.

3. A: Hello?

   B: Hello, Chen. This is Yuki. Did you finish your report for class?

   A: Not yet. I wanted to finish it over the weekend, but my Internet wasn't working.

   B: Oh, no. What are you going to do?

   A: I'm going to ask the teacher for an extension.

   B: What will you do if he says no?

   A: I guess I'll get an F.

   B: I hope he gives you an extension.

A

1. a　　2. b　　3. a

B

1. False　　2. True　　3. False

Making a Story Chain p. 83

Script

A: Can I borrow your book?

B: No, you can't.

A: Why not?

B: If I lend you my book, I will not read the book. If I don't read the book, I will not pass the test. If I don't pass the test, I will fail the class. If I fail the class, I will not graduate. If I don't graduate, I will not get a job. If I don't get a job, I will not earn any money. So that's why I won't lend you my book.

What would you buy?

Grammar p. 84

B

1. e　　2. a　　3. f
4. c　　5. b　　6. d

Listening p. 85

Script

A: Zoe, if a genie offered you three wishes, what would you wish for?

B: Hmm, that's easy. First, I would wish for ten million dollars. Then, I would buy a huge apartment in the center of the city.

A: Okay. That's a good one. What would your second wish be?

B: Hmm. I would wish for a great job. I would wish to be the CEO of a large company. I want an office on the top floor of a big building.

A: Okay then. You have one more wish.

B: Oh, I've got it! I would wish for three more wishes.

A: No fair! You cheated.

B: No, I didn't. You said three wishes.

A: Uh huh.

A

1. b　　2. b　　3. b

B

1. apartment　　2. top　　3. three

Muscles use a lot of energy.

Grammar p. 86

B

1. is　　2. tastes　　3. arrive
4. Do, get　　5. don't bite　　6. burns
7. see　　8. happens

Listening p. 87

Script

A: Isabelle, I'm going to take an early lunch. Can you help me with a few things?

B: Sure. What can I do for you?

A: If Mr. Parks calls, tell him to call me on my cell phone. I will keep my phone on at the restaurant.

B: Okay. Got it.

A: And if any of our customers call, tell them I am in a meeting. I will call them back when I return from lunch.

B: Anything else?

A: If my wife calls, tell her I'm really busy today, and I'm probably going to be home late.

B: You want me to lie, Mr. Winters?

A: No, no. Today is my wife's birthday. I'm taking my lunch break early so I can buy her some flowers. I'm going to surprise her this evening.

B: Oh, Mr. Winters. That's so romantic.

A

1. a　　2. c　　3. b

B

1. tell Mr. Parks to call him on his cell phone
2. tell the customer Mr. Winters is in a meeting
3. tell her Mr. Park is busy and will be home late

Murphy's Law

Reading p. 88

Comprehension Check

1. If something bad can happen, it will.
2. If you change lines, the previous line will move more quickly. / If you wash your car, it will rain.
3. It comes from Captain Edward Murphy.
4. He was in the Air Force in the 1940s.
5. The machines had problems.

Pair Work p. 89

1. e	2. d	3. a
4. b	5. h	6. c
7. i	8. g	9. f

Wrap-up p. 90

A

1. will drive	2. doesn't come	3. Will, eat
4. will, do	5. has	

B

1. would, be	2. got	3. won
4. did not have to	5. wouldn't share	

C

1. burns	2. cancel	3. don't bite
4. Do, grow	5. don't like	

Unit 9 Innovators

Warm-up p. 91

A

3, 5, 4, 2, 1

B

1. Marie Curie
2. Alexander Graham Bell
3. Thomas Edison
4. Leonardo da Vinci
5. Benjamin Franklin

Who was it invented by?

Grammar p. 92

B

1. Cars are sometimes stolen by thieves in my neighborhood.
2. The sandwiches for the party were eaten by John.
3. The driver that hit Sal wasn't seen by him.
4. The light bulb was invented by Edison.
5. A lot of damage is caused by tornadoes.

Listening p. 93

Script

Good morning, class. Today, I would like to tell you about two very interesting American artists.

First, let's talk about Shepard Fairey. Shepard Fairey is a famous street artist and graphic designer. Street artists use spray paint to create large paintings on the walls of buildings and on bridges. The paintings are seen by people who live in cities. In 2008, he made a painting of the former president of the United States, Barack Obama. This famous painting was seen by millions of people all over the world and made Shepard Fairey very rich and famous.

The second artist I'd like to talk about is Jeff Koons. He is a very famous sculptor. He creates sculptures that look like giant balloon animals. In 2013, his sculpture of a giant balloon dog was purchased by an unknown buyer for $58.4 million.

A

1. a	2. c	3. b

B

1. True	2. False	3. True

My Favorite Book

Vocabulary p. 94

B

1. author	2. animator / cartoonist
3. curator	4. graphic designer
5. inventor	6. sculptor
7. app developer	8. street artist

Listening p. 95

Script

A: Hi, Ms. Parker. I'm Officer Phillips. How can I help you?
B: My car was stolen this morning.
A: Did you see the person who stole your car?
B: No, I didn't.
A: Where was your car stolen?
B: It was stolen at the supermarket. I parked my car in the parking lot. When I came out of the store, my car was gone.
A: I see. Can you give me some information about your car?
B: Sure.

A: What type of car is it?

B: It's a four-door sedan.

A: What color is it?

B: It's green.

A: What year is your car?

B: 2012.

A

Police Report

Car Type four-door sedan

Color green **Year** 2012

Location of Crime supermarket

B

1. morning
2. not seen
3. supermarket

Script

A: Hello?

B: Hi, Ms. Parker. This is Officer Phillips. I have some good news.

A: Did you find my car?

B: Yes, we did.

A: Did you find the person who stole it?

B: No, we didn't.

A: Where did you find it?

B: Your car was found two blocks from the supermarket.

A: Two blocks?

B: That's right. But there isn't any damage.

A: That's good. Can I get my car?

B: Yes, but we need you to come to the police station. You have to sign some papers.

A: Okay. I'll be there in 30 minutes.

C

1. True
2. True
3. False
4. True
5. False

Solar Energy

Grammar p. 96

B

1. about
2. of
3. by
4. about
5. of

Listening p. 97

Script

1. A: Did you hear about the George Washington Bridge problem in New Jersey?

   B: No, I didn't.

   A: The bridge is used by more than a million drivers each day. They live in New Jersey but commute to Manhattan.

   B: Wow, that's a lot. What's the problem?

   A: The bridge isn't big enough. More lanes are needed. It takes too long to cross the bridge during rush-hour traffic.

2. A: What kinds of food are eaten in Thailand?

   B: Thailand has lots of different food. For example, it has a lot of tropical fruit like pineapples and mangos.

   A: What kind of meat is eaten there?

   B: Mostly chicken and pork. Beef is quite expensive.

   A: I see.

3. A: This university has a nice gym. What sports are played here?

   B: Well, men's and women's volleyball games are played here. And men's basketball games are played here, too.

   A: Where are women's basketball games played?

   B: Our school doesn't have a women's basketball team. Only volleyball.

A

1. c
2. b
3. b

B

1. True
2. False
3. True

I am my own boss.

Reading p. 98

Comprehension Check

1. He designs logos, signs, and other images.
2. He is designing a logo for a startup.
3. He works 4 to 5 hours when he is not busy.
4. If Kyle doesn't work, he doesn't get paid.
5. He tries to take one week in winter.

Wrap-up p. 100

A

1. The table was moved into the kitchen by Peter.
2. The clarinet is not played by his daughter.
3. Is classical music listened to by the students?
4. The Tesla sports car was invented by Elon Musk.
5. A lot of damage was caused by the flood.

B

1. The money was stolen by the thief.
2. The bike was stolen.
3. The wallet was stolen.
4. The shirt was stolen.

C

1. for
2. of
3. with

4. at 5. with

D

1. Bicycles are made of metal and rubber. They are ridden by cyclists.
2. Keys are made of metal. Locks are opened by keys.
3. Pens are made of metal and plastic. Letters are written with pens.
4. Glasses are made of glass and plastic. Glasses are worn by people with poor eyesight.

Unit 10 Gadgets and Technology

New Phone

Grammar p. 102

B

1. have, lived, for 2. has, known, since
3. have, studied, for 4. has, been, since

Listening p. 103

Script

A: What are you doing, Don?
B: There's something wrong with the television.
A: What's the problem?
B: The picture quality is really bad.
A: Maybe the settings are incorrect.
B: I don't think it's a problem with the settings. I think it's just an old television.
A: Should we fix it?
B: No. I think we need to buy a new one.
A: How long have we had this one?
B: Hmm. Let me see. We bought it in 2008. So we have had it for a long time.
A: Then it's time to buy a new one. Do you want to go to Tech Mart this weekend?
B: Sure. But this time, we're going to buy a bigger television.
A: Yeah. And one with a better sound system, too.

A

1. b 2. b 3. a

B

1. False 2. True 3. False
4. True

I lived in Paris for two years.

Grammar p. 104

B

1. has lived 2. was 3. have, played
4. dated 5. has studied 6. ate
7. have gone 8. have been

Listening p. 105

Script

1. A: Congratulations, Francis. You're engaged!
B: Thank you. It's exciting.
A: How long have you been engaged?
B: About three weeks now.
A: Can I see a picture of you two together?
B: Sure. I have some pictures on my phone. Here you are.
A: Wow. You make a cute couple. Where did you ask Bethany to marry you?
B: I asked her to marry me in Central Park.
A: How romantic!
2. A: How long have you been dating Tom, Erica?
B: We have been dating for six months.
A: How did you meet him?
B: We were in the same class. I had a crush on him for weeks.
A: When did you start dating?
B: He asked me out on the last day of class. But he did it in a text message.
A: A text message? That's funny.
3. A: How long have you been married, Stephanie?
B: I've been married for ten years.
A: How did you meet your husband?
B: We met online.
A: Cool.
B: How about you, Richard? Are you married?
A: I was married for two years. But I got divorced last year.

A

1. b 2. b 3. c

B

1. in a park 2. weeks 3. was

I had already bought this one.

Grammar p. 106

B

1. had, turned off 2. had studied 3. had, gone
4. Had, played 5. had, left

Listening p. 107

Script

A: Northwest Internet Services. How may I help you?
B: Hi. My name is Carol Freeman. I have a problem.
A: What's the problem, Ms. Freeman?
B: I've recently ordered Internet service from your company. But the technician didn't come to my house to install it.

A: Hmm. It says here the technician went to your house at 1:00 p.m., but no one was home.

B: Oh, no. I had already left my house when he came.

A: Would you like the technician to go to your house again tomorrow?

B: Sure.

A: How about tomorrow at 10:00 a.m.?

B: Okay.

A: The technician will be there tomorrow at 10:00 a.m.

B: Great. Thanks!

A

1. Internet 2. hasn't 3. tomorrow

B

1. False 2. False 3. True

Video Games and the Future of Gaming

Reading p. 108

Comprehension Check

1. Gamers enjoyed playing games on Nintendo and PlayStation.
2. They now connect to the Internet.
3. FPS games have become popular.
4. They download the software.
5. The person wears VR glasses.
6. It has become less expensive.

Wrap-up p. 110

A

1. for 2. since 3. for
4. since 5. since

B

1. have been 2. was
3. haven't seen 4. worked
5. have been married

Unit 11 I'm Stressed!

I'll help you.

Grammar p. 112

B

1. leaves 2. Does, open 3. isn't playing

C

1. will open 2. won't win 3. is going to work

Listening p. 113

Script

A: This is Janine. Please leave a message after the beep.

B: Hi, Janine. This is Cynthia. I need to talk to you. I have a really important interview tomorrow, but I'm so scared. The interview is for the sales manager position at Freemont Industries. This is my dream job. I don't know what I am going to wear. I don't know what I'm going to say. I'm kind of freaking out. The interview is with the sales director. I'm meeting him in his office at 11:00 a.m. I've worked so hard for this job. I really think I will get it. But I can't relax. Please call me when you get this message.

Script

A: Hello?

B: Cynthia. It's Janine.

A: Janine, thank you for calling me back. I'm so nervous.

B: Don't worry. It's normal to feel nervous about an interview. Just remember that you are the best person for the job.

A: Do you really think so?

B: Yes, I do. Now listen up. You are going to wear your black skirt, white blouse, and black jacket. I'm sure that will look good.

A: Okay. But what am I going to say?

B: Don't worry about what to say. You just have to answer the sales director's questions with confidence.

A: Confidence, right! Do you really think I'll get the job?

B: Absolutely. I know you'll get this job.

A: Thanks. I feel much better.

B

1. True 2. False 3. False
4. True 5. True

Pair Work p. 113

A

	Problems	Offers
1.	It's hot in here.	I'll open the window.
2.	This box is too small.	I'll get you a bigger one.
3.	I need to go to the airport.	I'll give you a ride.
4.	It's too heavy.	I'll help you.
5.	We are out of milk.	I'll get some.
6.	I can't hear the music.	I'll turn it up.

The Honeymoon

Listening p. 115

Script

A: How was your Christmas, Annie?

B: It was great, Brian. How was yours?

A: Mine was great, too. What's your new year's resolution?
B: I've thought about it a lot. I will quit smoking.
A: That's great. I've been worried about your health.
B: Me, too. But I'm worried I won't be able to quit though.
A: I know you will.
B: What's your new year's resolution?
A: I will read one book per week.
B: That's 52 books in a year!
A: I know. But I love to read.
B: I like reading, too. But that's a lot of books.
A: I can do it. I know it.
B: I'm sure you will. Good luck!

A

1. a 2. c 3. c

B

1. False 2. True 3. False

I'll be living in Canada.

Grammar p. 116

B

1. will be playing
2. Will, be studying
3. won't be attending
4. Will, be celebrating
5. will, be going
6. will, be doing
7. will be getting
8. won't be calling

Listening p. 117

Script

A: Shilo, can I ask you a question?
B: Sure, Sam. What do you think humans will be driving in 30 years?
A: Hmm. That's a good question. I think we'll all be driving electric cars.
B: Do you think we'll be driving flying cars?
A: Flying cars? No, I don't think so. That sounds dangerous.
B: What do you think we'll be eating 30 years from now?
A: Let me think about that. What will we be eating 30 years from now? Hmm. I think all of our food will be organic.
B: Organic? Yeah, I agree. What kinds of clothes will people be wearing in 30 years?
A: Oh, man. I have no idea. I don't even know what clothes look good now. I have terrible style.
B: Me, too.

A

1. b 2. a 3. c

B

1. False 2. True 3. False

A Record Deal

Reading p. 118

Comprehension Check

1. They live in Brooklyn, New York.
2. Their next concert is this Friday.
3. They have been together for five years.
4. They are going to play for 10,000 people.
5. He thinks the band will be selling out shows for 50,000 people or more.

Wrap-up p. 120

A

1. arrives 2. Does, open 3. is taking
4. isn't meeting

B

1. will close
2. will get
3. Are, going to visit
4. is going to apply

C

1. will be eating
2. Will, be studying
3. won't be living
4. Will, be celebrating
5. will, be traveling

Unit 12 Big Life Changes

Warm-up p. 121

A

1. a 2. c 3. e
4. b 5. d

Driving in a New City

Grammar p. 122

B

1. excitedly 2. rudely 3. loudly
4. well 5. happily 6. hard
7. comfortably 8. clearly

Listening p. 123

Script

1. A: Life in a new city is hard.
B: I know. I don't know where anything is. I'm completely lost all the time.
A: How long have you lived in Manila?
B: One month. I moved here in April.
A: I've only lived here for three weeks. Let's take a walk around the city together. Maybe we can learn the streets of the city more easily together.

B: Good idea.

2. A: The baby is crying again.
   B: She's crying loudly. She must be hungry.
   A: What time is it?
   B: 3:00 a.m.
   A: I'll do it. You were sleeping so peacefully.
   B: Thanks. I love y . . .
   A: Wait. Where's the bottle?
   B: Huh, what? Oh, it's in the kitchen.
   A: Thanks.
3. A: This apartment is huge!
   B: I know. I can't believe the company gave us such a big apartment in downtown Bangkok.
   A: This city is so cool. But everything moves so quickly. It's kind of scary.
   B: It's a busy city. But the people have treated us so kindly.
   A: I agree. Remember that Thais don't shake hands. If you want to greet someone politely, you have to *wai* and say, "*Sawatdee-ka*."
   B: Okay. I'll remember.

A

1. b 2. a 3. c

B

1. True 2. False 3. False

Our New House

Grammar p. 124

B

1. everywhere 2. downstairs 3. indoors
4. outdoors 5. around

C

last year, last week, yesterday, (today), tomorrow

Listening p. 125

Script

A: Look at all these boxes. What are we going to do?
B: Let's start by moving the boxes into the correct rooms. I wrote letters on the boxes so we would know which rooms they go in. This box has a "K" written on it, so it should go in the kitchen.
A: And this one has an "L" and an "R," so it must be for the living room.
B: Let's move all these bedroom boxes upstairs first.
A: But they're too heavy for me. I don't think I can carry them.
B: Okay. How about if you check the letters on the boxes, and I'll carry them to the correct rooms?
A: Good idea. This one has an "O" on it. I can't remember what the letter "O" is for. Hmm.
B: It's probably for my office.
A: Oh, that's right.
B: My office is downstairs. I think I'll carry that one last.

A

1. moving in 2. letters 3. heavy
4. office

B

1. True 2. True 3. False

You'll Get Over It

Grammar p. 126

B

1. get on 2. get on with 3. get in
4. get off 5. get over 6. get out

Listening p. 127

Script

A: Hello?
B: Mitch, it's Karen.
A: Hi, Karen.
B: I want to know how you are doing at your new job in India.
A: I'm doing okay. Delhi is a lot more crowded than Minnesota. And a lot hotter, too. I felt the hot weather as soon as I got off the plane.
B: You're lucky you are not here in Minnesota right now. It's minus ten degrees Celsius. I want to get out of here! So tell me about your new job.
A: Well, I'm an executive for a textile company here. We supply textiles to more than two hundred companies worldwide.
B: That's great. Have you had a chance to get out and see the city?
A: The company has taken me to dinner a few times. The food is incredible.
B: I love Indian food.
A: Me, too. But there's a lot to learn at my new job. I spend most of my time at the office. I haven't spent much time walking around the city. I'll have more time to do that later.
B: I'm glad you're doing great. It was nice talking to you.
A: You, too. Thanks for calling, Karen.
B: Bye.
A: Goodbye.

A

1. c 2. a 3. b

B

1. Minnesota 2. 200 3. dinner
4. hasn't

Tim's Tiny House

Reading p. 128

Comprehension Check

1. He has lived in a tiny house since 2009.
2. He had to pay a lot for heat and air conditioning.
3. The tiny houses use less energy and take up less space.
4. He has solar panels. / He uses solar power.
5. He has to pay for telephone and Internet service.

Listening p. 129

Script

Good afternoon, everyone. Thank you for inviting me here to share my story. About ten years ago, I decided my family and I needed to make a change. We were not living responsibly. We were wasting a lot of food and electricity. So as a family, we decided to start recycling. But we didn't feel satisfied. There was more we could do. We stopped eating meat and became vegetarians. Raising animals for food creates a lot of air pollution. We also feel better because we started eating more healthily. But we decided to do more, so we sold our gasoline-powered cars. And we bought an electric car. Our electric car runs on batteries, not on gasoline. But we weren't finished yet. We were living wastefully. We decided to install solar panels. Last summer, my sons helped me put solar panels on our roof. Now, our monthly electricity bill is very small. And we're helping the environment!

A

3-2-1-4

Wrap-up p. 130

A

1. loudly	2. softly	3. hard
4. well	5. beautifully	

B

1. indoors	2. around
3. upstairs, downstairs	4. outdoors
5. everywhere	

C

1. get in	2. get on with	3. get off
4. get out	5. get on	6. get over

MEMO

MEMO